WHO ATE ALL THE PEREPLOTKINS?

And Other Tales From Derby County's 2008/9 Season

By Edgar Smith

www.ramspace.co.uk

PURE PHASE PUBLISHING

First Published by Pure Phase Publishing
88 Manor Road, Derby, DE72 3LN

Copyright © Stewart Smith 2009
All illustrations Copyright © Samantha Smith 2009
All rights reserved

This book has been published independently and is in no way affiliated with Derby County Football Club

Any comments, enquiries, or feedback should be sent to s_spaceram@post.com or visit www.ramspace.co.uk

ISBN: 978-0-9561144-1-9

ACKNOWLEDGEMENTS

First of all, thanks to everyone who bought the first book Bad Worse Worst, especially those that contacted me with praise and encouragement.

A massive thanks also to those who helped me to sell the book or bought multiple copies for friends and relatives – Robert Lane, Carl Walker, Simon Kirk, Lisa Sayers, Richard Cromwell, Keith Winter, Mark Brown and Caroline Heaton. Also to Eagle Books on Derby Market and Soccerbooks who took a small stock of the first print.

Thanks to Mum and Dad for the encouragement, sales and Dad for proof reading the first draft. Thanks also to my brother Chris Smith for all the support and help, especially with the on-line sales.

Finally, huge thanks to my wife Samantha for all the support from day one. Sam supplied all the illustrations for this book and didn't once question the wisdom of publishing an esoteric Derby County book during a recession!

Introduction

In the summer and autumn of 2008, I began piecing together Journals I had written for the Derby County website Ramspace, to form the basis of a book about The Rams' record breaking relegation in 2007/8. I eventually self-published the book under the title "Bad Worse Worst – The Story of Derby County's record breaking 2007/8 season".

The book was never intended to be a statistical or journalistic account of the season but was meant to reflect the experience of being a Rams supporter during that year; what we talked about and what we felt. In its own modest way, the book represented a small slither of history that would otherwise have been lost as we roll onto another season.

The book sold modestly – enough to recoup costs and pay for another print – but it did appear to strike a chord with particular niche of Rams fans. Fans who enjoyed some laughter in the dark; an eye for trivial detail; and a healthy irreverence for the shiny world of modern football.

I received several encouraging and supportive emails from people I'd never met and I realised that what I was writing several times a week wasn't just floating off into cyberspace unnoticed. I also unexpectedly received a request from 442 magazine to review the book and even more unexpectedly, received a 4/5 rating. To this day, I don't know how the 442 link came about. The recurring question was often "when's the next one out?" and it's for this very reason that the book you are reading exists today.

I hadn't planned to follow up Bad Worse Worst but I must admit that I thoroughly enjoyed the whole experience so didn't need my arm twisting too much! However, the last thing I wanted to do was test the goodwill of all the friends and family who supported me last year. As a result, I've opted for a small print-run to once again produce a small slice of Rams history for those much loved strangers who have requested it.

I sincerely hope you enjoy what is to follow…

Edgar Smith, Derby, Summer 2009

After Paul Jewell's rebuilding in the summer of 2008, some suggested that the squad was now a bit top heavy

PART 1

"We have got 19,000 season ticket holders for next season. All I can say to them is that we will get promoted next year. I am pretty certain of that with the team we are looking to build and the players we are looking to bring in."

Paul Jewell April 2008

After Derby County's disastrous 2007/8 Premier League campaign, it was clear to all concerned that a massive turnaround was required for The Rams to bounce back. Manager Paul Jewell and Chairman Adam Pearson had been working hard to give the squad a face-lift, a task which had begun several months earlier when the Rams Premier League season had been written off as a lost cause.

During the close season, Jewell wheeled and dealed and had brought in 14 new faces by the end of August to add to his signings of the previous January (Savage, Villa, Sterjovski, Carroll and Stubbs). A similar number of players departed, including the previous years top scorer Kenny Miller and club Player of the Year Darren Moore. Jewell did not spend heavily on transfer fees (the £1.7m paid for Rob Hulse being the highest) but acquired a lot of "free" transfers, such as Commons, Albrechtsen and Connolly, who would have commanded significant signing-on fees and lucrative contracts due to their contractual situation.

When the pre-season began, it was clear that the new-look Rams side still needed some tweaking. A 0-2 defeat to Dutch part-timers FC Top OSS was followed by narrow victories against three non-league sides (Burton, Mansfield and Rushden) and draws against lower league Rotherham and Oldham. The squad was well used so the best XI was still not clear. What was clear was that the centre of midfield was becoming problematic and The Rams had become embroiled in a very public saga surrounding the signing of Swansea's Dutch midfielder Ferrie Bodde. At one stage, Bodde handed in a transfer request and spoke publicly about his desire to join The Rams. However, the two Chairmen failed to agree a fee and on the eve of the season, The Rams formally withdrew their interest.

The midfield situation was compounded by the situation surrounding Robbie Savage. Alan Stubbs had been installed as the new Rams captain and Savage was barely featuring in the pre-season matches. The press frequently reported that Jewell was trying to move Savage on, whilst Jewell publicly questioned Savage's work-rate in training. Whatever was happening behind the scenes, Savage did not appear to be part of the plans.

A fortnight before the season kicked-off, Jewell's quest for a new midfielder led to the signing of Polish international Przemyslaw Kazmierczak on a season long loan from Porto, with The Rams paying a loan fee of around £400,000.

A week before the season began, The Rams hosted Dutch club FC Utrecht at Pride Park and drew 2-2. Seeing the Rams score twice in the same match was still a novelty after a season of torture but alarm bells were ringing as the opposition still scored too easily. The match also saw the debut of Latvian trialist Andrey Pereplotkins.

The Season begins

Derby County's 2008/9 season kicked off with a home fixture against Doncaster Rovers. Although Doncaster were regarded as a tidy footballing team, the fact was that The Rams had been two divisions above Doncaster the previous season. Rovers had been a non-league club as recently as 2003 and had not spent heavily on promotion. All things considered, Rams fans fully expected to begin the season with a comfortable, if not emphatic, victory.

The Rams fell to a deserved 0-1 defeat. Doncaster had won comfortably and it was clear that Jewell's rebuilding programme was far from complete. The Pereplötkins situation said it all; signed only two days before the season began, it was almost as if Jewell had forgot to write "right winger" on his shopping list, then dashed out to acquire one. Pereplotkins appeared only twice in the league for The Rams before vanishing from the first team picture (his season-long loan was terminated in January). It also showed Jewell's lack of faith in the likes of Gary Teale and Mile Sterjovski, both international right-wingers whose confidence would not have been helped by the episode.

The choice of full-backs was another puzzle for Rams fans. Jewell had acquired Paul Connolly from Plymouth and Jordan Stewart from Watford and sang the praises of both in the press. When the team ran out to face Doncaster, Tyrone Mears and Jay McEveley retained the full-back berths. Both were Billy Davies signings and integral parts of the Worst Team Ever.

Kazmierczak lasted less than an hour against Doncaster before being replaced by Robbie Savage. After being frozen out for much of pre-season, Savage was far from effective. Jewell's criticism of him in the press hadn't endeared him to Rams fans either, some of whom gave Robbie a torrid time.

Just to put the tin hat on the Doncaster debacle, new captain Alan Stubbs was carried off before the hour mark. It was disappointing to see the man Jewell planned to shape his defence around depart so early. What we didn't expect though was what happened next; a fortnight into the season, Alan Stubbs announced his retirement from professional football.

The Rams scraped past Lincoln City in the Carling Cup after extra time, (courtesy of a Nathan Ellington hat-trick) but league form remained weak. However, after a pitiful home defeat by Southampton, Jewell decided to make wholesale changes for the Carling Cup tie at Preston; Mears and McEveley were jettisoned for Connolly and Stewart, whilst Jewell pulled a rabbit out the hat with the inclusion of young defender Miles Addison in a central midfield role. Addison had made his Rams senior debut under Terry Westley in 2006 but had only played once more in the following two seasons. Whether Addison's inclusion was inspired or desperate, he was a revelation. Meanwhile, Paul Connolly had taken the captains armband. The Daily Mail, always the first for Derby County mischief making, had claimed that Jewell has pulled Connolly's name out of a hat for the captaincy. This was strenuously denied and Connolly retained the armband for the rest of the season.

Off the pitch, the revolving doors continued to rotate as Davies' US signings Eddie Lewis and Benny Feilhaber both left the club, soon followed by Gary Teale who joined Barnsley on loan. Teale had been expected to leave in the summer but there had been no takers. He was clearly not part of Jewell's plans. More intriguing was the loan of striker Liam Dickinson to Huddersfield. Dickinson had been signed only the previous month for £750,000 and The Rams had only scored once in the first four league games. Jewell said the move would allow Dickinson to play regularly but all manner of rumours circulated. Some simply said that he hadn't impressed in training; others suggested the city life had turned his head (Dickinson later went on to score 4 in 7 whilst on loan in the party capital of Blackpool!).

The August transfer window also included the farcical loan move of Tyrone Mears who joined Marseille. Mears flew to Marseille for an initial trial without authorisation from the club and was fined heavily as a result. Mears claimed that his agent had told him that permission had been given, whilst the club claimed that Mears had been expected at Moor Farm for training as usual. The player clearly preferred to be in Marseille than Derby, especially as Paul Connolly had won the battle for the right-back slot. The club eventually agreed a season-long loan for a fee of around £150,000, topped up by a fortnights saving on Mears' wages!

Through the entrance door came 18 year old Dutch midfielder Nacer Barazite from Arsenal. Barazite became the fifth player to fill the problematic right wing berth, following Pereplotkins, Davies, Green and Commons and the season was barely a month old.

361 days after Derby beat Newcastle

On Saturday 13th September, The Rams faced Sheffield United at home. A tough looking match but one Paul Jewell had to win. It would soon be a calendar year since The Rams last recorded a league victory and Jewell's reputation was already suffering without more unwanted statistics. Fortunately for Jewell, his team did not let him down, with Rob Hulse scoring the winner against his former club in front of a tea-time TV audience.

After the Sheffield United match, The Rams were no longer carrying a metaphorical losing monkey on their back. Draws against Swansea and Cardiff followed before The Rams faced QPR away on September 27th. QPR had been pre-season favourites with some bookmakers so this would be a real test for newly confident Rams. The build up to the match was over shadowed by a row over ticket prices. Only seven league matches had been played this season yet the QPR owners decided to hike up ticket prices by 33% meaning travelling Rams would be charged £40 instead of the already-quite-expensive £30. Derby refused to accept this (credit to the board here) and the Football League stepped in to adjudicate before settling in the Rams favour – QPR were not permitted to raise ticket prices once they had been agreed at the beginning of the season. The price rises also applied to QPR fans who were none-too-pleased and distributed protest leaflets outside the ground.

The QPR match would be my last before embarking on a three week holiday. Derby won the match 2-0 with goals from Martin Albrechtsen and Tito Villa. Suddenly promotion, or at least the play-off's, were back on the agenda –

The Rams were still 17th but only three points from sixth place. During my holiday, text updates informed me that The Rams' unbeaten run now stood at seven matches. I arrived back in the UK on the day Derby defeated Plymouth 2-1 at Pride Park. The Rams were placed 9th in the Championship but only a single point from the play-off places. A settled team was beginning to take shape and The Rams were in the winning groove – surely good times lay ahead, didn't they?

August 9th Derby County 0 Doncaster 1

"Where did we get that Perry Plotkins from?"

"Don't know mate, I thought he was the postman in Trumpton"

The Journals of Derventio – June to September 2008

Here are my scribblings from the first leg of the season. As The Rams season provides little inspiration, I seem more pre-occupied by Hull City's astonishing start to Premier League life!

June 16th

En route to Middlesbrough last season, Simon gave an enlightening speech about how the fixtures are not randomly generated at all but manipulated by dark forces to avoid any hotspots, for example teams with a big following will rarely have seaside Bank Holiday games. He concluded by saying "Blackpool away is a definite midweek game, or least in the middle of winter". I looked at the fixtures today and sure enough - Blackpool away Tuesday October 21st, hardly ideal for a lads weekend. I think that's the general idea.

June 29th

A one liner from the Hull Fan At Work: "I went to a conference at your place the other day (i.e. Pride Park). There's some optimism there isn't there? As soon as I stepped in the lift it said 'Going Up',". Boom! Boom!

July 5th

I've been telling anyone who'll listen all week that I'm really pleased with the signing of Liam Dickinson and would much rather sign a young player on the way up than give an old journeyman a last pay day.

I just read the new New Boys* piece on him: signed for a couple of grand from non-league; scored a load in his first full season; tall but doesn't score many headers; doubts about moving to a higher level. Have we just signed Phil Gee? Obviously by that I mean he'll score 15 goals and we'll get promoted.

New Boys – an article on Ramspace where a fan from the previous club provides a write-up on our new signing.

July 7th

I read the story linking Forest with Pearo today (Derby Telegraph website) - I make that Earnshaw, Holmes, Oakley, Nyatanga and now Pearson linked with a move there. Two points to make here: 1) Forest must have the laziest scouts in the world. 2) If they're not careful Forest could end up with half a team from the Worst Team in the World E*vv-eeeer!* (or more accurately, players mostly deemed not good enough for said team).

If you're reading Mr. Calderwood, Andy Todd is still available.

July 10th

I don't know who Ruben Zadkovich's agent/ PR person is but he seems to have J-Mac's pointless story slot on the Telegraph website truly sewn up. Not bad for a player who most Rams fans (including me) couldn't pick out from an ID parade and has never kicked a ball in a Rams shirt. I know the summer can be a bit slow for footie news but do we really need "Ruben has an Olympic Chance", "Zadkovich named in Aussie Olympic squad", "Ruben set for Messi challenge in Olympics" and "Zadkovich confident Aussies can claim Olympic medal"- when one paragraph could surely have covered all? (There are a similar number of stories regarding his Aussie debut, not to mention signing and post-signing). Without such filler there could have been space for more interesting pieces such as "What does the future hold for McEveley (and/or Mears)?", "Mo Camara discovered in cupboard at Moor Farm" or "So what *did* Craig Brown do?".

July 16th

Wondered why the transfer frenzy has slackened off a bit? According to the Hull Fan At Work (who has recently become a prisoner of his newly acquired Sky Sports package) Jagger *(Paul Jewell)* has been taking part in David Seaman's Celebrity Golf on Sky. A quick internet search reveals this to be the David Seaman Safe Hands Charity Golf Classic 2008, with an entry fee of £6750 per team, £3000 of which goes to charity. A good networking opportunity I'm sure.*

*Joking aside, in the much quoted Stan The Man autobiography, Stan Ternent lines up several deals whilst trawling the bars of Magaluf on a end of season jolly and bumping into various players and managers en route.

July 17th

Maybe Jagger did learn something from Stan Ternent - one minute the gaffer is playing Pro-celebrity golf in the Algarve, the next we've signed a midfielder from Porto *(Kazmierczak)*! (see previous entry).

July 25th

The Hull Fan At Work showed me a piece from the Daily Mail that was basically a day in the life of Phil Brown, starting with Brown driving from Bolton to Hull at 5am on the phone - "like minded souls are up at 5am" apparently. Phil throws in no end of management speak, climaxing with the bullshit bingo winner of - "If I was 24/7, I'd end up flatlining". We both scratched our heads over this one before concluding it must mean something involving Class A drugs.

July 27th

(Written regarding Mansfield v. Derby in pre-season)
Not long now. Despite the warm weather, yesterday finally felt as though the summer break was coming to an end and football season was on its way. The first sign was when my neighbour asked if there was a game on today. When I asked why, she replied that when she had passed the train station at 8:30am, there was a visible Police presence as well a group of lads holding cans of Stella. It's nice to have an early start but would the pubs even be open when they reached Mansfield?

July 30th

It doesn't take much for a managers reputation to disappear (is Mike Newell still alive anyone?) and Colin Todd has undoubtedly been on a slippery slope for, well, has he ever not been? A poor spell at The Rams was followed by an equally bad one at Bradford that left the Bantams heading for League Two (i.e. the fourth division) and Todd with his P45 in hand. Todd resurfaced at little known Danish side Randers FC, a club whose ground holds only 12,000 and have spent most of their history outside Denmark's top flight. Well, "he has to make a living somehow" you may think. But wait...according to World Soccer, Todd is the second highest paid manager in Danish football earning an astonishing £265,000 p.a.! How did he manage that? Bryan Robson and Peter Reid are on the Ryanair website as we speak, eyeing up flights to Aarhus.

August 3rd

I went to the Utrecht game on Saturday; it was nice to see the Rams score twice in less than a month but despite all the new signings, I was left feeling that there's a lot more work to be done. I don't usually analyse the team on the Journals but I'll go stick my neck out and say that the midfield needs sorting out pronto!

World food inflation has also hit Pride Park; the new "Meal Deals" included a soft drink and fries at £3.50; and Cheeseburger, fries and soft drink for £6.40. I presume pies must be available somewhere but not on any of the displays with the menu taking a definite American twist (hot dogs, burgers etc). Beer is also up with a pint of lager costing £3.30 (I think it was £3 last year but I drink bitter so I'm not sure). I knew inflation was creeping up but didn't know it was at 10%. It's fair to say, I won't be in the ground before five-to-three very often.

Simon got a free ticket for Saturdays match. Like thousands of us, he received his season ticket last Saturday in a cheap unmarked envelope (my £435 purchase was in the junk mail pile for a couple of hours until I got round to sorting it out.) Unlike most of us, Simon received two season tickets. Instead of going straight on ebay, he rang the club to let them know and was told that he should send it back immediately by recorded delivery! After politely asking why he should go to the Post Office and fork out for their mistake, a compromise was reached with a prime West Stand ticket- he didn't get a Meal Deal thrown in though.

August 10th

The following entry follows the first-day-of-the season 0-1 defeat to Doncaster

What a complete and utter let down yesterday was. Defeated by a team who were two divisions beneath us last season and have actually lost players rather than gained them. Most of you would have seen the match but some of you wouldn't, so here's a few questions raised by yesterday:

Why sign two new full backs if they aren't going to improve the first team? The left back slot is the most puzzling; according to Jewell we tried to sign Jordan Stewart in January as well. If all we want is a Championship reserve left back we might as well have kept Mo Camara. If Stewart and Connolly are signed to play - get them in.

The Robbie Savage situation has been a disaster. Fair enough Jewell didn't play him against Utrecht or Mansfield but leaving him out of the low key games (including Hull behind closed doors) seems completely counter-productive. When Savage was thrown in yesterday he was evidently not up to speed. The fans slated him, Savage's confidence and desire will take a hit and the midfield is still a problem. Not the best bit of management.

Pearson and Jewell have often said that we've been building for next season from as early as January last year and had a massive head start over Reading and Birmingham who didn't discover their fate until the last day. This being the case, why was Pereplotkins pitched in after an hours mediocre display last week?

In fact, did we learn anything from the Utrecht game? My analysis to my brother was: "neither Pereplotkins nor Kazmierczak are ready yet; we still concede easy goals (McEveley implicated in both); the midfield is basically not right; we didn't have a shot in the second half." We sent out exactly the same team yesterday and exactly the same things happened.

Finally, a big concern at the moment is the style of football. We are still not creating anything with our best chance yesterday being when a defensive howler let Hulse in. We didn't up the tempo at all at 0-1 and there was no pressure or bombardment of the Doncaster goal. Again, too reminiscent of last season for comfort. The tactic seems to be head-height passes to the wing at the moment and I can't see that keeping us entertained for long.

On the bright side, first day results have proved to be meaningless in the past and certainly when we've had a good season, the first match has been poor. In fact, looking at the season following our last relegation, beating Reading 3-0 on the first day proved to be completely misleading and left us thinking everything would be fine for months after. At least now we know we need to sort things out.

Another bright spot was the £2 a pint offer before the match. After saying last week that I wouldn't be in the ground before five-to-three very often, I was outside at 13.29 shouting "come on, I know you're in there" to the bar staff. Well, slight exaggeration but at least I saved a couple of quid.

August 13th

The following entry refers to Derby's 3-1 a.e.t Carling Cup victory over League Two Lincoln at Pride Park.

Thank God we've finally got a win of sorts, if not only to give Jagger some respite in his press conferences. He's said a few times about being "as bored of saying it as you are of hearing it" and I noticed after Saturday he used a new tactic of throwing a few stats in. First off he quoted Hull and West Brom's respective starts to last season before adding that we had 135 points to play for and could afford to drop 42. Fair comments but it says something about his optimism for the Doncaster match that he had them ready to trip off the tongue.

The second example was a few selective match facts from the Donny game: apparently "we hit exactly the same amount of passes as Doncaster" (completed passes is the more common measure), "had 51% of possession" (not at all impressive for home favourites in my view) and finally "got in their box 53 times against their 15" (a quick check reveals shots on target to be equal).

It all smacks of saying "come on, we didn't get *hammered* by Doncaster". At least you can get good odds on us to beat Bristol City; which I'm fully confident of us doing now we know where the net is.

August 17th

A few weeks ago the Hull Fan At Work had an award to collect and turned up smartly dressed, "grey trousers, brown shoes - it's the Phil Brown look" was his comment. In reply I asked if that's what you do after turning 40 - forget replica shirts and dress in homage to the manager.

Last season Paul Jewell dressed almost exclusively in 90's hooligan chic - mostly Ralph Lauren jumpers and shirts. Results were poor but his clobber would have done his credibility no harm with gentlemen of a certain lifestyle. But what the hell was Jagger wearing yesterday? A high sleeved t-shirt with what looked to be a lycra bodysuit underneath, coupled with tight trackie bottoms. He looked like an extra from a bad 80's sci-fi show. Please don't let this look catch on with blokes in their forties.

August 20th

Did you notice that for their latest publicity stunt, Paddy Power are paying out on Stoke to be relegated after Stoke lost at Bolton on Saturday? This is apparently going to cost them around £30k - far less than an advertising campaign in the national press I would imagine. As a self-proclaimed "Silver Lining" offer Paddy are giving Stoke season ticket holders a "no-strings" £50 free bet.

I wonder how many of Stoke fans used this to have a punt on Stoke to stay up?

August 24th

The following entry was written after the 0-1 home defeat to Southampton.

This time last year, almost to the day, we were sitting outside the same pub, drinking the same beer preparing for what we thought would be the Rams first win of the season - Birmingham at home. What followed was complete disappointment with an extra dash of pessimism for the season. The only difference yesterday was that Simon wasn't wearing flip-flops. One of our conversations in the pub was - when was the last time the Rams won at home on a Saturday? We thought it was probably Cardiff at home in the promotion season. I've just checked and it was. March 17th 2007. To put it into perspective, my son who is now happily walking around, has never seen his dad come home happy on a Saturday. Come to think of it, he probably thinks I've got some crappy part time job where I leave the house and return a few hours later in a bad mood.

I'm doing the Times column again this week so I'll write about the game then but it would suffice to say that the mood isn't good. Last night I was settling down for a bit of Reading/ Leeds festival coverage when my phone rang. The Observer wanted a comment about the match as the Derby fan who had offered was now refusing to answer his phone!

Column written for the Times on-line following the Southampton match:

If you think Derby have problems, take a look at Southampton: a team who avoided League 1 on the final day; a manager recruited because of financial constraints; closing down parts of the ground because of finances; only two survivors from last seasons curtain closer; a mish-mash of kids and freebies (that's cast off "free" not Bosmans). Derby were absolutely played off the park by Southampton on Saturday. How did that happen?

For starters, Derby have signed 14 players over the summer, yet only five new faces started Saturdays match. The team featured two tried and untrusted full backs (Mears and McEveley), even though we've signed two more who were praised to the hilt by Jewell on signing. Two left wingers (we currently have two international right wingers *(this refers to Teale and Sterjovski but forgets Estonian international Pereplotkins)* - one scored a screamer for his country midweek - both are currently *persona non grata*) and we dropped a striker who has scored three of the clubs four goals this season *(Ellington)*. We didn't even have a right winger on the bench with the previous man jettisoned from the 16 *(Pereplotkins!)*.

I hate to be negative but talking about Derby at the moment, it is simply telling the story. I think it was Steve Claridge who compared Birmingham's pre-season training under Barry Fry to Zulu Dawn - 40 blokes running down the hill. Well, that's how Derby are at the moment. Jewell commented that we were thin at the back this week after Stubbs' premature retirement - we only have six central defenders (Davis, Albrechtsen, Leacock, Nyatanga, Todd, Addison- plus those whose CV states "anywhere across the back"). We also need "more competition in centre midfield" yet Jewell has already signed at least four who could be his middle two.

Of course it will take time for a new team to gel but we don't seem any closer to knowing what this team might look like. The disappointing thing is that we were told in the summer that our preparations would be months ahead of Birmingham and Reading and we would have a real head start. Looking at the league table, we are already eight points behind Birmingham.

Management and players have commented that the added pressure from the crowd is making it difficult to play at home. Saturday's crowd was down by 6,000 and that would surely not go unnoticed by the bean counters (although Soton brought far less than Doncaster). If it falls any lower, Jewell might be feeling pressure from more than the crowd. We have sold a lot of season tickets but with only a couple of thousand ticket sales a fortnight, we'd struggle to even cover Savage's wages for the month.

As the game finished, Noah and The Whales "Five Years Time" played across the tannoy. Was that a subliminal plea for patience from the American marketing experts or am I just being paranoid?

August 27th

"I picked the wrong team, so I'm as much to blame but I'll sort it out, it's my job to do just that. I'll make changes."
Jagger after Saturdays match? No, this was our old pal Stan Ternent after Huddersfield's 1-3 home defeat at the weekend. Come on Stan we've just lent you a £750k striker*, sort it out!
Liam Dickinson

August 31st

At least one Rams player scored yesterday - Liam Dickinson scored a glorious overhead kick for Huddersfield. Unfortunately for Stan Ternent, Huddersfield went on to lose 2-1 at Millwall. Watching "The Championship" this morning, a few other ex-Rams appeared: Matt Oakley scored for Leicester; Danny Graham bagged a hat-trick for Carlisle; and Marco Reich nearly burst the net for Walsall. By far the most popular ex-Ram this weekend must be Kenny Miller who scored a brace in the Auld Firm match. As documented in the Journals last May, Rangers fans were chanting against him before he'd even signed - I wonder what his popularity rating was today?

September 1st

A truly shocking site at the Hull v Wigan match on Saturday - no, not the Hull defending but Phil Brown's 'tache. Brown looked like he was auditioning for a part in spoof cop show Beef 'n Onion, or even as an extra in Jagger's next homemade film.

I asked the Hull Fan At Work today and apparently it's all in a good cause. Raising awareness of testicular cancer after Hull reserve 'keeper Matt Duke had a scare.

Duke has had an odd career. He signed for Hull for £20,000 from Burton Albion in 2004 when Hull were in League 1. Despite playing only 8 games in 4 years for the Tigers he has ridden in the slipstream of Hull's success to become a Premier League no.2.

(The Hull Fan At Work thought I was having a dig at Matt Duke here – it wasn't the intention, I just thought it was an interesting career. Duke became Hull's no.1 for a spell later in the season with his 13 games more than doubling his career appearances to date.)

September 3rd

The marketing men have really got their work cut out after the start to the season we've had. How to put a spin on two home defeats in two matches? The official website proclaims that we are at least top of the league when it comes to crowds in the Championship. "What a load of rubbish, we've only played two games" you might think...but wait. The table reveals our average home gate to be a full 10,000 higher than Forest. That's the kind of stats we like!

September 7th

When Phil Brown was sacked by the Rams, he couldn't buy a days work. One job he was close to getting was that of Bournemouth manager. I would imagine it wasn't exactly the dream gig for northern Phil but a salary nonetheless. He was pipped by Kevin Bond, partly due to the ex-Pompey assistants's relationship with Bournemouth sympathiser 'Arry Rednapp and the promise of a few good loanee's. A few of 'Arry's young reserves arrived and - I'm making an assumption here - didn't set League 1 on fire.

We're all well aware of what happened to Phil Brown but what about Bournemouth? Last week Kevin Bond was sacked. He taken them into the fourth division and they began the season with a 17 point deduction due to their chaotic finances. They are currently second to bottom on minus 14 points. In retrospect, probably not best appointment.

September 10th

Last Sundays Observer had an article about the Baseball Ground. On the subject of the famous pitch it said "...a notorious mudheap. Players complained about the pitch constantly; the mud was dense and sulphurous, rich with decades of industrial waste, and grass died fast"

It's a good job nobody carried out a risk assessment on doing a slide tackle with an open wound through sulphuric industrial waste. The ground would have been closed in no time. Fortunately, no-one had thought of Health and Safety in the 70's: men operated industrial machines with bare hands - with a fag in one of them; women in high heels stood on swivel chairs to reach heavy files on top of cupboards; and The Rams won the League Championship twice

If you're an ex-player whose body parts have started turning green and dropping off, contact your local No-Win No-Fee solicitor today.

September 14th

Written following the home victory against Sheffield United

Like all good things, all bad things must also come to an end. So thank god that yesterday we finally won a league match. I can sympathise with Jagger to some extent; all the records were becoming an albatross around the neck of the club - although the sympathy only goes so far - he had far more chance to do something about it than you or me. When discussing Jewell, you could not ignore the stats. It reminds me of two academics debating the merits of Communism in the USSR. One bloke would always answer "yes but what about the 20 million killed?" until the other finally said "stop going on about the 20 million!" The point is - you can't. And you can't ignore no victories in nearly a year.

Now we can move forward and stop every match preview dredging up the next unwanted record (when did we last win away in the league by the way? - no, let's move on). The Observer even saw it fit to take us on one last trip down misery lane, by listing all 36 winless matches - thanks.

September 17th

The QPR match is only 10 days away and there are still no tickets available (QPR's fault I believe). Even the R's website doesn't offer the chance to buy any. We booked the train to London a couple of months ago but the rumour is that tickets are £40 each. There is definitely a spilt vote on whether to go to the game or not at that price. As the Jackal said on seeing QPR chairman Flavio Briatore - suntanned, open necked shirt, hairy chest and shades - on Sky Sports - "there's no way I'm giving him forty quid". (The day out in London isn't in doubt).

September 18th

Things aren't improving for Stan Ternent up at Huddersfield. After their latest defeat he came out with the ultimate abdication of responsibility "it's not my fault, it's the players fault". Not what the chairman wants to hear I'm sure. I remember Bryan Robson saying something similar last year - let's hope Stan doesn't meet the same fate.

The QPR ticket row has hit the press today - QPR are trying to charge us £40. For the purpose of comparison: Simon's friend in Basle had a book of three Champions League tickets last week - Barcelona, Sporting Lisbon and Shaktar Donestk. The total cost was less than £60.

The following entry is a pre-QPR Times online column:

Overshadowed by the Newcastle saga and the usual Big Four coverage, the story of Derby refusing to sell QPR's marked up match tickets made few headlines. It might be a storm in a tea cup but it could also lead to an FA ruling with wider implications. At the time of writing and the game six days away, no tickets are available for the away end whilst the FA decides if QPR can raise ticket prices by 30% mid season.

A group of us bought train tickets to London two months ago but after hearing the proposed £40 ticket price, there's now a divided opinion on the best way to spend £40 in London. Even at the original £30, some are having second thoughts. On seeing QPR's playboy chairman Flavio Briatore, the archetypal medallion man surrounded by models on TV, one mate commented "there's no way I'm giving him forty quid", another friend is reluctant to subsidise Naomi Campbell's corporate champagne.

So now we have to make a few decisions. None of us are keen to pay £40 for a ticket; and after all the hassle, most of us are reluctant to put anything into the QPR coffers. On the other hand, as a loyal fan, it pains you to think of the away end being empty; it's no good for the players and no way to support the club.

One justification for not going could be that we are "boycotting" the game. Boycotting is often questionable in football - I've heard many a part-timer credit their non-attendance to protest when the chips are down. Having bought train tickets, we could make a valid claim to be boycotting - just don't expect to see us outside the ground waving placards.

For some readers, this may all sound hypocritical coming from Derby. Last season after selling out of season tickets, Derby held their own fans to ransom over the remaining tickets by hiking up matchday prices by around 50% in a move unchallenged by either the compliant local media or supporters groups. Matches against Sunderland, Portsmouth, Bolton and Birmingham were all classified as "Gold" under the bling-coding which indicates the degree to which the club profit from any given game. Inevitably, away fans were fleeced. Rest assured though - The Rams reaped every ounce of bad karma going.

Derby's stance comes only weeks after the Falkirk and Rangers row in Scotland (the Auld Firm clubs are charging opponents 5% to sell away tickets - Falkirk told Rangers to stick it and sold the tickets locally). Dundee United had less luck when Celtic threatened to block similar tactics, risking around £100k of gate money for United. I suppose market forces will always dictate to some degree, so with a top price of £50 in the Championship, it will be interesting to see how many full houses there are at Loftus Road this season.

September 24th

According to the BBC, one of the reasons given by QPR for the ticket rise was "to provide a better standard of entertainment for home and away fans". The rationale being that QPR will be able to sign more, better quality players. Is it possible to simultaneously entertain the home and away fans? Using the same logic, did Portsmouth fans feel thoroughly entertained after being drubbed 6-0 by

Robinho and the gang at Man City? Or did Doncaster fans feel ripped of by the poor quality of entertainment at Pride Park in August? Towards the end of last season, maybe the ticket office should have been saying "it's pretty shocking in there to be honest mate, just give us a fiver". Sometimes, the logic of business just doesn't work in football.

September 26th

Now the working week is over I can focus on the QPR trip. Who's bringing what for the train? What to eat and where? Who's going to the game and who isn't? The Jackal is apparently "masterminding" the drinks for the train - I'll be well disappointed if he just turns up with a few cans of beer after that build up.

There'll be six of us on the train tomorrow, no doubt with a couple of drinks. Over the summer, I was on the other side of the fence so to speak. On the train to Leicester, sober and with my wife. Elsewhere on the train was a group of lads (returning from a stag do). We heard a bit of a commotion and tuned round to see one of the party, who wasn't particularly petite, being pushed into the overhead luggage rack by his fun-boy mates. To make matters worse, he was only wearing an over-the-shoulder "Borat" bright green thong. Not a pretty site. To be fair, it was all harmless but I suppose the moral of the story is "please show consideration for other passengers".

I've got a long haul flight on Sunday with two legs of seven hours each. All with a 16 month heavyweight champion on tow. Remind me of this if you see me in Shepherds Bush tomorrow.

September 28th

Written following the QPR match

QPR were pre-season favourites to win the league with some bookies. We completely nailed them yesterday. This was due in no small part to our new found passion and desire that has been missing for as long as I can remember. Both managers commented about the Rams continually winning the second ball and it was ironic that the QPR DJ played Duffy's "Mercy" (*"I'm begging you for Mercy"*) on the final whistle. Four particular examples stood out:

- Paul Connolly's goal-line block when Blackstock had an open goal. Last year, or even last month, the striker would have tapped it home and the full-back would have shrugged "it was an open goal from two yards- what could I do?". "Defend like your life depends on it" is the answer.
- Miles Addison had two 50-50's with QPR's giant Jamaican defender Damien Stewart and completely (and legally) destroyed him both times. Stewart didn't know what had hit him and was sent spiralling towards the nearby BBC studio's for his own version of *Strictly Come Limping*.
- Tito Villa should wear a headband every week. After getting kicked in the face, he looked like a South American freedom fighter and duly waged guerrilla warfare on the QPR defence; culminating in him forcing the corner for his goal. He still hasn't scored with his feet though.
- Despite not being in the matchday 16 once this season, Mile Sterjovski was at the front of the queue for congratulating the players and clapping the fans. Decked out in Rams polo shirt and trackie bottoms, you'd have thought he had scored the winner. (this may have something to do with the large Aussie community in Shepherds Bush. Perhaps Mile didn't want to disappoint his fan club).

Sheffield United wasn't a false dawn and things are finally looking up. Could we be top 6 when I return from holiday?

Rams fans adjust expectations as the season progresses.

"I fancy 4 or 5 nil against Doncaster today. Who have Birmingham got?"

"Watford will be a tough game, I'd take a point. Who are Barnsley playing today"

PART 2

"Progression is going forwards. Going backwards is regression. Going sideways is just gression"

Noel Gallagher May 1994

The Rams seven game unbeaten run came to an end with a 2-3 defeat at Blackpool. However, the momentum was not completely lost as the Rams were unfortunately held to a draw at Coventry and beat Norwich comfortably at home 3-1. November began with the eagerly anticipated home fixture against Forest. Forest were having an awful season and were second from bottom with only nine points from 14 matches. The Rams were only two points from the play-off places and form suggested that Rams fans could be in for a treat. An emphatic win would give a huge stamp of credibility to Jewell and could be the moment when the previously disjointed group of players finally became a team to be proud of.

The game was a massive letdown from a Derby perspective. The Rams could not repeat the fluency of the Norwich match and went 0-1 down before Tito Villa's scrambled equaliser made the scores level. The end of the match was mired in controversy after the Rams had a perfectly legitimate header from Miles Addison ruled out (this is not my biased take on events, TV analysts pored over the replays and could find no fault); whilst Nacer Barazite had an injury time penalty saved. To make matters worse, the jubilant Forest 'keeper was Derby born ex-Ram Lee Camp who celebrated wildly with the Forest fans after the match.

The match was completely over shadowed by the events of the closing minutes but the fact is that the last minutes should not have mattered. Forest were a team bereft of form, confidence and quality, as their league position confirmed. The Reds also played the last 20 minutes with 10 men after the sending off of Lewis McGugan.

Following the Forest match, the Rams recorded only one league victory in November and one in December. The poor form in the league was in part masked by an impressive run in the Carling Cup. The run was driven by the cup form of Ellington and Villa who shared the six goals scored in victories against Brighton and Leeds, adding to Ellington's earlier hat-trick against Lincoln. The pair continued to struggle for goals in the league but had fired the Rams into a Carling Cup quarter-final tie away at Premier League Stoke City. It should be noted that Villa and Ellington's cup goals had all been scored against lower division opposition which suggested the level they might excel at.

On a freezing December night, the Rams defeated Premier League Stoke 1-0 at the Britannia Stadium. Stoke's long ball tactics were meat and drink to new boy Darren Powell who was in his element with the ball in the air (more on Powell later). Partnering him that night was on-loan West Ham defender James Tomkin who later that season became a Premier League regular back at his host club. The winning goal was scored in injury time courtesy of an unbelievably cool penalty by Nathan Ellington. As the whole ground bit their nails, Ellington waited for the 'keeper to commit before passing the ball gently to the centre of the net. Cue mass delirium from the travelling support.

The end is nigh for Jewell

Despite the euphoria of the Stoke match, the prevalent feeling amongst Rams fans was that we were no longer moving forward. Jewell had brought more than 20 players to the club since his appointment but he appeared no nearer to having the side he wanted. Both full-backs who started the season were now out on loan (Mears at Marseille, McEveley at Preston); Robbie Savage had been dispatched to League One Brighton for a month; and two of the most expensive summer investments – Kazmierczak and Ellington – were regularly warming the bench. Meanwhile, Gary Teale (not in the top five right wingers in August) had returned and was back in the first team frame.

Jewell still continued to add to the squad. One of the most curious signings was that of defender Darren Powell. Powell was 32 years old and had been without a club since being released by Southampton in the summer. He had spent the vast majority of his career in the Championship or below. Jewell's rationale for the signing was that The Rams had injuries in defence and Powell was experienced and available. Fair enough. However, the whole episode raised a few questions amongst Rams fans. Firstly: Derby still had experienced defender Andy Todd under contract and collecting a significant wage. Jewell had always maintained that Todd was simply not part of his plans and it was nothing personal. Darren Powell was of a similar age to Todd and had a far less impressive CV., yet Todd had not even featured on the bench this season. Andy Todd joined League One Northampton on loan a few weeks later. Supporters also wondered what the future had in stall for Lewin Nyatanga. Nyatanga had played almost a full Championship season on loan with Barnsley last year and had amassed over 20 caps for Wales. Powell was now preferred to Nyatanga.

In fairness to Powell, he wasn't the worst player to be seen this season and his commitment was always exemplary (his performance at Stoke in the Carling Cup was truly magnificent). The problem was that he represented a definite change from the vibrant young side Jewell had envisaged to short-termism in order to stop the rot that was setting in. After eight Rams appearances, Powell was released when his two month contract expired. He played only four more times that season after joining League Two Brentford.

If Jewell's attempts to solve defensive problems were questionable, his solutions for The Rams striking problems were equally desperate. Since January 2008, Jewell had invested heavily in strikers: Tito Villa had cost £2m; Rob Hulse £1.7m; Nathan Ellington £1.5m for a season loan; and Liam Dickinson

£750,000. Other Jewell signings Sterjovski, Commons and Davies were also billed as being able to play "down the middle". With Villa and Ellington still struggling to score league goals and Dickinson dispatched once more on loan (this time to Blackpool), Jewell spent the last of the transfer kitty on Charlton striker Luke Varney. Varney joined initially on loan with a permanent transfer agreed when the January transfer window opened, for a fee of around £1m. Varney had signed for Charlton for around £2m after an impressive season with Crewe but had struggled at Championship level, scoring eight in his first full season and just two in the current campaign – as a result his value had depreciated by half and he was no longer a regular in a Charlton side in the relegation zone. Was this the man who could save Jewell and The Rams season?

Varney did score on his home debut but the Rams were defeated 1-2 at home to Crystal Palace. The Rams limped towards the Christmas fixtures until the home match versus Ipswich on December 28th. The match was an uninspiring 0-1 defeat to a mediocre Ipswich side. The following day, Rams fans were greeted by the following official statement from the club:

"Derby County can confirm today that the club has parted company with manager Paul Jewell with immediate effect.

Paul has taken the decision to leave his role as he believes it is in the best interests of the club, and feels that he is no longer in a position to take the club forward.

It is with great regret that we accept this decision and Derby County would like to put on record its thanks to Paul Jewell for his effort and commitment over the last 12 months.

Assistant manager Chris Hutchings will take charge of the club with immediate effect and will lead the team for the next two fixtures, away to Forest Green Rovers in the FA Cup and at home to Manchester United in the Carling Cup semi-final."

Paul Jewell November 2008 – December 2009

DERBY 0 VILLA 6

ANDREJS PEREPLOTKINS

NEWS OF THE WORLD SEX SCANDAL

STAN TERNENT

11 POINTS

DERBY 0 DONCASTER 1

SAVAGE IN EXILE

NO PREMIER LEAGUE WINS

Sept '04

Thanks for the memories

Journals of Derventio - October to December 2008

Written after returning from my annual jaunt to India and The Rams unbeaten in seven matches.

October 19th

I didn't get out and about too much over the past few weeks, so not a lot to report. I could only find one footie channel available on the TV package and that was MUTV.

I did stumble across one oddity though. Last season Dean Sturridge was the "summariser" on Radio Derby and generally regarded as rubbish*. He left at the end of the season - it wasn't clear whether he was axed or he just gave it up as a bad job. A fledging media career over before it began, right? Wrong. On a rare night out in Bangalore, I saw a bit of West Brom v. Fulham on Star Sports Asia. Guess who was co-commentator? Studger. The ironic thing is that the strongest thing on his C.V. would be "experienced Premier League commentator for the BBC". Good luck to him though, in previous years I've heard all manner of Aussie cranks who make Studger look like John Motson (in his heyday).

*When he first started, I remember saying that I rated Studger in his analyst role. After a couple of listens, it became clear that his crash course in media training had only given him a dozen phrases to be repeated at regular intervals.

October 21st

I'm almost up to speed with three weeks of Rams news but the most significant stat is that we were unbeaten whilst I was away. Last time I went away for a spell, we were also unbeaten and went top of the Championship with a win at

Southend- I distinctly remember the text from my brother- "new signings look immense" (i.e. Fagan, Teale, Pearson).

One of the more bizarre stories was the match fixing scandal against Norwich. It sounds like a richer more Malaysian version of the Jackal texted a load of his equally rich mates saying "Norwich 11/8 with Harry Wong. Derby won once away in 2 years. Definitely worth £100k". In a bar later that night, his mates claimed they'd only had a couple of quid on, whilst weeping into their bottles of Tiger beer.

October 22nd

Text received yesterday: "That slag Lee Camp has signed for Forest" *(Lee Camp had signed on loan).*

Camp was saying on the Telegraph website that he'd received some "good natured stick" from Rams fans. On the left was excerpts from the site Forum with a thread titled "Camp = JUDAS" He was getting called all the names under the sun and his Rams career was torn to shreds. I expect he'll get some more cheeky banter on November 2nd.

October 23rd

When the QPR ticket row was going on, QPR played down the accusations of overpricing by saying that all the tickets in their £50 Platinum section had been sold. Why were the Rams moaning about a measly 40 quid? So it was interesting to read a QPR fan in When Saturday Comes saying the following "The empty seats in the £50 section suggested that all the season ticket holders had gone on holiday together, or that the club had crossed the line from spin to outright lies".

October 26th

Simon was in Corporate for the Coventry match on Saturday; on Friday we speculated about who would be the next person to join the "stalkers gallery" on his phone (for new readers, this already includes Giles Barnes, Brian Lara and Steve Howard amongst others). Would it be Cyril Regis? Lloyd McGrath? Sean Flynn? The lucky man photographed with Simon's arm around him was...Mo Konjic.

After the match he had to endure a speech from one of the Coventry Directors who told the amassed freeloading businessman "it's you people who are the future of the club". Don't tell any Cov season ticket holders if you know one.

In other conversation on Friday night, I was talking about the extracts from Ted McMinn's autobiography published in the Telegraph. One of the stories was about when Ted lost his rag with Marco Gabbiadini during a training session. Ted had been named in the squad for the Bass Vase along with a collection of reserves and kids. When training finished, Marco commented "Can you collect the bibs and balls for the first team Ted?". This went down like a knackered lift with the self proclaimed "old-hand at mickey taking", who launched himself at Marco with a flurry of windmill arms.

We thought it was a classic one liner by Marco with Simon's shoulders bouncing up and down in laughter for minutes after.

October 29th

The following was written after the 3-1 home victory against Norwich.

Last night was the first match I've been to since going on holiday and it felt like watching a different team - the match stats say it all really: 22 shots (11 on target) and 12 corners. Having a corner or a shot every three minutes is Burley-esque levels of entertainment! Even Chocolate Wrists *(Stephen Bywater)* has turned into Iron Wrists with an outrageous one-handed diving save in the second half. Two points from the play-off's with bottom of the league at home next* (although I just checked and they're not bottom any more. Even more worryingly, we've lost to the other three in the bottom four already this season). **Forest*

After the match, the Jackal said he was pleased that Forest had won. His reasoning? "if they'd had lost tonight, Calderwood would be out. I'm a great believer in stats and teams who have just sacked their manager usually get a result in the next match. Also, shit teams don't win twice on the trot away from home". Good logic, especially the latter point.

October 30th

It sounds like things aren't going much better for Stan at Huddersfield. Here are some choice quotes from a BBC story where poor old Stan gets more desperate as he goes on:

'Huddersfield Town manager Stan Ternent has told BBC Radio Leeds that there is no need to panic over their current league position.
"We're playing quite well but everything at the moment seems to be going against us…I would prefer to be travelling to Carlisle on Christmas Day in charge of Huddersfield Town. But if I'm not then I'll have my Christmas dinner at home, so what is there to panic about?… Don't worry about me - I'm OK… I left a good job to take this job - they paid me more money than I'm paid at Huddersfield - but it's a challenge… the fans want to pick the team. They can't pick the team - I pick the team, that's what I'm paid to do." '

November 1ˢᵗ

Just to clarify: in the October 29th entry when I wrote "Burley-esque entertainment", I meant football in the style of George Burley; rather than "burlesque", which is defined as "a humorous and provocative stage show featuring slapstick humour, comic skits, bawdy songs, striptease acts, and a scantily clad female chorus". Although I'm sure the latter is also entertaining in its own right.

November 2ⁿᵈ

Written following the disappointing 1-1 draw with Forest. The text refers to Miles Addison's disallowed "goal".

There's probably nothing to add to what everyone's thinking about the Forest match. I got a text afterwards from a Watford mate, Big Nick, saying "the referee's a disgrace" followed shortly after by "the header at the end - after about ten minutes analysis nobody could find out why it was disallowed".

After having a couple of hours to calm down, the biggest pity was that the Rams we saw on Tuesday night didn't turn up* - then the last minute wouldn't have mattered.

*i.e. The Rams who beat Norwich 3-1

November 4ᵗʰ

It looks like Stan will be having Christmas dinner at home after all (see Journals October 30th). My favourite quote from the BBC story was when the Huddersfield chairman said the club had "a problem in attracting a manager with the whole package". Does the "whole package" mean the same as "a full deck" or "the full shilling"?

Can we have Dicko back now then please? We're a bit short up front.

November 5th

A bit of football trivia from BBC sport:

Q. Until David Beckham joins A.C. Milan in January, who is "the only English player appearing in the top flight of a major European league?"

A. "Marseille's as-yet unused squad member Tyrone Mears"

The following is a Times on-line column written after The Rams 3-0 away defeat to Reading.

Derby County: 6 Months On

Roughly six months ago, The Rams Premiership debacle reached its nadir with a 0-4 home defeat by Reading. After the match, I remember commenting that we hadn't been beaten by a Premiership heavyweight but a team we would be facing next year. If we intended to bounce back - we had to bridge a huge gap. Six months later, we lost 3-0 at Reading. So has anything changed?

The first observation is that only two players started both the Pride Park catastrophe and this weekend's game. Lewin Nyatanga and Tito Villa. If Dean Leacock had been fit and Villa not scored a Carling Cup hat trick in the week, it would probably have been zero. On top of that, the starting 11 contained only one of Jewell's many January signings- again yer man Villa. The likes of Savage and Sterjovski rarely make the 16 nowadays.

Despite Jewell and the Chairman saying that rebuilding started in January, the reality is that the Rams rebuilding really kicked-in at the end of August. If you want evidence - we started the season with a trialist ring-winger and he hasn't been seen since the summer (he was signed properly two days before kick off).

So where are the Rams now? Well, still not as good as Reading. But being "not as good as Reading" who average over three goals a game at home and boast the leagues top scorer is more comfortable than being "not as good as Reading (by a country mile)" who are third bottom in the Premier League.

All in all, the Rams are now a decent mid-to-upper table Championship side but with players who are improving constantly and in the main, young enough to do so. A far better picture than six months ago even if Saturdays scoreline doesn't suggest it. Even better, Paul Jewell has quietly taken the Rams on our best cup run for years and without wanting to jinx us, only a lower league side stand in the way of a quarter final place (it's Bradford, Huddersfield or one of those lot). *(We were due to play Leeds in the Carling Cup).*

November 10th

How's this for "hot off the press"; according to the Times website, a new book about corruption in football, called The Fix, reports on the suspicious betting patterns on Norwich v. Derby. That was only about a month ago, how did he get that written and published so quickly?

The author is apparently a "Canadian journalist academic" who recommendations are thus: "The FA and Fifa need a security department like US sports have, five or six tough former Scotland Yard or anti-mafia guys. People whose ideal is The Sweeney. Task them on drug-taking, anti-match-fixing."

Tough guys who like the Sweeney? I can't see Police HR putting that on the advert.

One thing that always baffles me about match fixing is that it's usually high profile players and matches, with huge bungs paid. Surely odds are odds whoever's playing? Why pay a hundred grand to Bruce Grobbelaar when a Scottish Third Division 'keeper will chuck one in for fifty quid and a deep fried Mars bar?

(I'm sure no lower league Scottish goalies *would* do this).

November 12th

The following entry was written following the 2-1 Carling Cup victory against Leeds

The pay-on-the-gate facility looked a bit of a "piss-up" and "brewery" situation last night. I wandered up to the ground in good time and saw a huge queue. "Thank god I bought a ticket in advance" I thought. As I went up to one of the four empty, unused turnstiles brandishing a ticket I was told by a Steward that I couldn't enter the ground here but had to join the big queue. I was completely stunned and rhetorically asked "seriously?". In this age of customer service, where the fan comes first, what do you think the reply was?
a) "Yeah sorry mate, it's just the way the turnstiles are set up tonight" (maybe with an apologetic shrug of the shoulders). Or
b) "DO I LOOK LIKE I'M JOKING!!!!!!!" (with matching aggressive stare).

No wonder Stewards rate somewhere between referee's and Traffic Wardens amongst the nation's favourites.

November 16th

The following entry was written after the impressive 3-0 home victory against Sheffield Wednesday

After a few days fever, I thought a couple of hours in the fresh air wouldn't do me any harm yesterday afternoon. Here are a few observations from the match:
- Claude Davis seems to be turning into a cult hero - a kind of Igor on Lilt. The turnaround has been pretty quick but quite a few people around us have suddenly warmed to him. The mood where we sit is quite good for gauging *"the general consensus"*. I suppose his general buffoonery is funny

when you're winning 3-0 in the Championship but less so when its 0-0 in the Premier League.

(Looking back, I don't know what inspired the above comment but it's fair to say that Davis' stock fell from this point on).

- Where did McEveley suddenly re-appear from? *(He'd been on loan at Preston)* As the Jackal pointed out, "if you come back after a month nowadays it means you're shit doesn't it?" I look forward to McEveley vying with Zadkovich for the pointless filler pieces in the Telegraph. This week, I fully expect to see - "Jay- I'm back to fight for my place". I less expect to see "Jay- I was thrilled when Jordan Stewart scored a 25 yard screamer...honestly".

- Are we getting that used to winning that Pride Park is turning into the Emirates? Instead of cheering the lads to the finishing line, an Arsenal style exodus was taking place during the last ten minutes. As the final whistle went, the players congratulated each other, shook hands with the opposition and then turned to clap the fans. The problem was the stands were almost completely deserted. As the Jackal and I disappeared down the empty staircase, I'm sure Barazite could be heard shouting "thanks for coming lads, I really appreciate it, see you against Preston yeah?...yeah?...yeah?...lads?".

November 18th

With Hull City hovering around the European places, memorable victories at Spurs, Arsenal and Newcastle; and sold-out signs at the KC Stadium; which pressing issue was the subject of the Hull City Times on-line column this week? It was titled "Has Anyone Seen Nathan Doyle?" No great revelations though - in summary: signed from The Rams; was in the reserves, starred in the play-off's, now back in the reserves. There is hope for him though. Look what happened to

the last Rams youth team full-back-cum-midfielder who ended up at Hull - Tigers captain Ian Ashbee. Give it ten years Nathan, you'll get there.
(Nathan Doyle subsequently made three Premier League appearances for Hull. Not bad for saying we only got £50k for him).

November 19th

I had to smile at the BBC story about Andy Cole's retirement last week. On the right hand side was an archive story titled "Cole eyes 'ideal' end to career" about him signing for Forest. The first quote regarding his retirement was Cole saying "It's not an ideal ending..." Nice to keep the theme going.

According to the Mirror a couple of weeks ago, it all came to a head after the Forest v. Ipswich match where the match stats showed that Lee Camp had covered more ground than Cole. The journalist was actually sticking up for Cole by pointing out that he was subbed midway through the second half. Come on though; let's look at an average passage of play. Camp collects the ball, runs from the six yard box and boots it - twelve yards covered. A striker should be challenging for the header or anticipating the second ball. If possession is won, the striker should be ending up in the box with or without the ball. He would then return to the half way line when the move breaks down. A round trip of around 100 yards. How many times would that happen in a match? All while Camp is in his box. It wasn't as if Forest got hammered, the match ended 1-1. Calderwood said it was best they went their separate ways. Cole is just leaving the car park as we speak.

November 21st

Despite leaving the Rams many months ago, the cult of Stan Ternent lives on. The phrase "Stan Ternent" is now an adjective at work meaning "old school or heavy-handed management". Recent examples of usage include: "I heard the meeting was a bit rough?", "well, it was going alright until Fred went a bit *Stan Ternent* about hitting the targets". Or "did you read that email I sent the team? Was it ok or do you think it was a bit *Stan Ternent?*"

The following entry is an article written for the Times on-line:

The Decline and Fall of Andy Todd

When 32 year old debutant Darren Powell sliced a clearance into the path of grateful Ipswich striker Jonathan Walters, it showed quite how difficult Paul Jewell's search for defensive cover has been. Powell was, by Jewell's own admission, far from match fit having been released by Southampton in the summer and a free agent since. Jewell had been thwarted in his attempts to land someone on loan and Powell was one of the few options available. One option was to call "come in number 22 - Andy Todd" but Jewell has not even hinted that this might happen.

Andy Todd's Derby County career has thus far been a complete disaster. Ironically, it began in the best possible way. A solid performance in midfield, capped by a spectacular headed equaliser in a 2-2 draw against Portsmouth in August 2007. Within a month though, Todd's fall from grace had begun, culminating in a shocking performance in a 6-0 defeat at Anfield. Todd disappeared with an unspecified back injury after the game although rumour mongerers suggested a post match discussion with Billy Davies also meant he would never play for Davies again.

Todd made his Rams comeback under Jewell for an FA Cup tie versus Sheffield Wednesday. According to Jewell, the Rams were short of defenders and Todd offered to help out - much in the style of a bloke in the pub on Saturday night offering to play left wing the following morning. Todd remained in or around the Rams first team for the remainder of the season. Bafflingly playing (poorly) at right-back in the latter stages. It was only before the final match of the season that Jewell announced that Todd was not part of his plans and dropped him. Why that didn't happen a dozen games earlier is anyone's guess.

Jewell has attempted to completely rebuild the Rams this season but has never been too proud to play anyone he thinks might do a job. Of those thought to be "not part of the plans", Pearson and Bywater have seen transfers collapse to return to the first team; Savage has had his chance; Teale has returned from a loan spell to start a run of matches; even Claude Davis has been a regular. But still no Andy Todd. It's almost comical when the local paper reports team news and says "Leacock and Albrechtsen are still injured so Nyatanga and Davis remain the only ft defenders at the club". Mentions of Todd being out of favour stopped months ago.

However, the news is that he is still alive and has played recently in behind-closed-doors friendlies. His wages seem prohibitive for a loan move and the Darren Powell episode says all you need to know about his Rams career. Will he ever kick a ball professionally again? Who knows.

(Within a day of writing this article, Andy Todd joined League One Northampton on a month's loan)

November 24th

The Hull Fan At Work pointed out an article about Phil Brown on the Times website today. In it, Phil Brown makes the following intriguing claim about his time at Derby:

"I wanted to bring in someone like Brian Horton [now his trusted no. 2 at Hull] to help, but that wasn't allowed. If I'd had the backroom staff I have now, I would have taken Derby into the Premier League."

Firstly, I wonder why he wasn't allowed to bring in "someone like Brian Horton"? I can't imagine Horton was commanding a huge salary (he was managing Macclesfield at the time). Without wanting to indulge in libellous speculation, I would guess the name "Murdo McKay" may be found in the answer. He was Director of Football, how could he not be involved?

Secondly, given Phil Brown's recent success, you can't blame him for tarting up his Derby debacle a bit. But surely an assistant manager isn't worth 20 league places? We weren't exactly on the cusp of greatness when Phil left us. Having said that, 59 year old Horton might have performed better than Dean Holdsworth as a makeshift centre forward.

November 26th

(The following entry was written after a freezing cold midweek draw against Preston)

I received a text yesterday afternoon that finished "...in Siberia with a pint of Guinness watching VH1" to which my reply ended "...in Swadlincote drinking a cup of tea". Four hours later I felt like I was in Siberia and listening to VH1.

The Jackal couldn't make kick-off yesterday so instead of the usual "see you outside at half past...[an hour later]...make it 20 to - it's freezing" I was in the ground to hear some of the pre-match build up. I don't know if the stadium DJ suffers from ADHD but he played at least four songs in about two minutes. It was like being drunk at home and thinking "this is my favourite song of all time" (30 seconds later) "No, this is my favourite song ever" (another 30 seconds and a swig of booze) "no this is my favourite etc., etc..." He started with a burst of the Piranha's (der-der-der-de-de), then a bit of "Bloomer", then "Clubbed to Death" and finally "White Riot". Why don't they just put a drumbeat under the lot, shout "One O'clock, Two O'clock, Three O'clock Rock!" between songs and call it the Jive Rammie megamix?

The two blokes in front of us come out with some rubbish but I've got to give credit for the comment on Tito Villa: "he's going to get sent off in a minute - he's tackling like Hong Kong Phoey" which he absolutely was. The previous best was probably "who they bringing on next - Rolf Harris?" after Zadkovich and Sterjovski joined the fray against Leeds.

November 30th

The Hull Fan At Work told me a bizarre statistic a couple of weeks ago - Mr. o.g. is Forest's top goal scorer in the league this season. There have been three matches since and this still remains the case.

This means that Tito Villa's contribution for Forest *(he scored an own goal in the November 2nd fixture)* puts him in joint third on "1"; with o.g. on 3 and a few others on 2. Villa is in a similar position for the Rams with league goals; joint third and tied with a selection of defenders. The main difference is that he's four goals off the pace for Derby, whereas he's only one behind any one of Forest's blunt-shooters. Another player to outscore Andy Cole this season for Forest is Youl Mawene.

In addition to all this, Liam Dickinson has only played 15 minutes of Championship football but has now scored two league goals at this level (for Blackpool on Saturday). As good as any Forest striker, the same as Villa and one more than Ellington. Bizarre stats all round.

(I refrained from calling Ellington "The Duke" but on the other hand, a nickname basically meaning "a lower ranking member of the monarchy" is quite fitting for someone becoming very rich for doing very little).

December 1st

After yesterdays generally negative stats, I think I should counterbalance it with some more upbeat figures.

On the eve of the Carling Cup quarter final, it's worth noting that Ellington and Villa have scored nine Carling Cup goals between them in just six starts this season. Both are also in an exclusive club of Rams players who have scored hat-tricks this Millennium. I think Lupoli is the only other member (before that you would have to go back to Simmo).

More than 4,000 of us will be going tomorrow night so let's hope the run continues.

December 3rd

What a tremendous night at Stoke; for me, it was comparable with the Play-Off final for sheer excitement of how it all happened.
It wasn't exactly the best start. We were a few minutes from the ground just after 7 O'clock but were still a few minutes away at five to eight. Horrendous traffic and having to park miles away meant Rams fans were still streaming in well after kick-off. My seat was near an old acquaintance who greeted me with the standard to a latecomer - "we're winning 5-3 mate". I was further disorientated to see an unfamiliar face warming up for the Rams - Mo Camara. I could have repeated the greeting I'd just given "how you doing mate, haven't seen you in ages". Mo's credibility went up immediately when he started berating a linesman for a throw-in decision. Despite being here for about five minutes in two years, Camara had already shown more passion for the club than half of last year's team.

The first half could hardly be called a classic; standing there in sub zero temperatures I had to comment "it's going to be great standing here watching penalties at half eleven tonight". Looking at Zadkovich warming up (in every sense of the phrase) I couldn't help wondering if he was dreaming of Bondi

Beach. If it had have been Stoke in the Championship, December, freezing, dreadful game and nil-nil, I probably would have been thinking "what am I doing here?", "where's my life going?" etc. As it was, we were still in with a chance of our first semi-final in my living memory.

The second half was a different story altogether. The Rams were the better team by miles and could have won it several times. I think you probably know what happened in injury time.

A special word for Gary Teale here*. He's not had the best of seasons and has really been a scapegoat where I sit. For example: Teale makes a tackle on the half-way line, the ball goes in to touch - "F-ing hell Teale, we're playing in white"; Norwich's Centre Half heads home from a corner - "it's like playing with ten men with Teale" (obviously it wasn't Teale's man); it goes on. Teale came on as sub in the 90th minute, probably as fresh legs for extra time. He's not even been in the 16 recently but he came on psyched up and ready. The Rams won a corner and Teale could have seen out the game. Instead, before I could say to Bob "why's Teale wearing gloves *but* a short sleeve shirt?" Teale, with maybe his only touch of the game, took the corner whilst tired Stoke were napping. Kaz whacked the ball at Griffin; the ref thought "I'm not staying here for another half hour"; Griffin observed the "respect" campaign and said nothing. It was then all down to the man I just love to call "The Duke" to finish the job. The rest is quite literally history.

(Yes, credit to Teale but I should really add that Powell, Tomkin and Addison were absolutely immense last night).

I must take credit here for possibly the only positive Gary Teale comment made in 2008.

The following is a Post-Stoke Times on-line column

Cup Fever

When it comes to Cup success, Derby County have defied the law of averages over the past twenty years - and not in a good way. Despite spending all of that time in the top two divisions of English football and half of it in the top flight, Derby had, until Tuesday night, never reached a major semi-final (i.e. not including the Anglo-Italian Cup).

A simple comparison with our dear friends and neighbours, Forest and Leicester, shows you just how appalling the Rams record is. Since 1988, Forest have reached two FA Cup semi-finals and one final; three League Cup finals and won the League Cup twice. Leicester have reached the League Cup final three times and also won it twice. If you really wanted to rub our noses in it, you could point out that even our County cousins Chesterfield have out performed the Rams by reaching the F.A. semi-final in 1997 (a historic all Derbyshire semi-final was prevented when Derby choked in the quarter finals against Middlesbrough at the Baseball Ground).

So that's why Derby County fans were absolutely ecstatic after beating Stoke during the week. The Carling Cup might not be everyone's priority but with a distinctly mediocre league campaign and after last years debacle, it's just what the Doctor ordered. The victory over Stoke was left very late but after hitting the woodwork twice and dominating the second half, it was fully deserved.

We are now faced with the small matter of Man United in the semi-finals. The Rams fans I spoke to had divided opinions before the draw; Burnley would theoretically give us the best chance of Wembley (despite being hammered 3-0 by them last week); whilst Man United would be a near write-off for progression but would bring in 100,000 fans and plenty of TV cash over the two legs. Not to be sniffed at with the transfer window on the horizon. (Tottenham weren't really discussed).

For Paul Jewell, the Cup will be a welcome diversion. Ask anyone how Cardiff did last season and the answer will be "they got to the FA Cup final"; few people outside Wales will remember their league position. After Saturdays awful home defeat by Crystal Palace, Jewell might also be hoping that league performance becomes an afterthought when judgement is made.

December 4th

I thought it was time to give an update on the Journals book - Bad Worse Worst.

I started off with a small print-run of 150. Thankfully, I've now sold most, mainly through word of mouth sales and repeat sales (i.e. people coming back for multiple copies, often with Christmas in mind). It was never intended to be sold in shops but after the initial burst of sales I thought I'd try and take it a step further and get an ISBN number and barcode (required to sell in most shops). Now, you would imagine that in the anti-corporate bohemian world of literature, it's all easy come, easy go. That couldn't be further from the truth. Would you believe that in order to sell a book in Waterstones, I have to sell and dispatch to a third party in Sussex, for them to deliver to Derby? Postage aside (and multiple copies are very, very heavy and expensive to post), I could walk to Waterstones from my house in twenty minutes with a rucksack of books on my back. I feel like a farmer next-door to Tesco being told "sorry sir, we only buy our potatoes from Egypt".

The main hurdle I'm up against is people saying "I bet it's all doom and gloom, why would I want to read that?". Maybe a more upbeat title would have done the trick. The only thing I can say in defence is that it's not doom and gloom. Don't forget we also had Jagger in the News Of The World, Earnie in his Hummer and Bob Malcolm on the M1 - not to mention the Nuts awards. Basically, it's wall-to-wall Journals. If you like the Journals, you'll like the book. If you don't get the Journals then I wouldn't bother (that's why I'd never make it in sales).

I'm getting a reprint before Christmas with the ISBN number on and the book is now available on Amazon. Amazon had unbeknown to me listed it themselves and are offering to "source a copy" for £1.99. Bizarre - they're all in the boot of my car.

Commercial break over - now back to the footie.

December 7th

After Saturdays rubbish *(a 1-2 home defeat to Palace)*, I decided to milk the Stoke game for the Times column. Here are a couple of additional observations about last Tuesdays match:

There was a story about Stoke midfielder Glen Whelan in the week, saying how he hoped his Carling Cup performances would help him get into the first team. Whelan was completely dominated by Addison on Tuesday - I remember saying afterwards that had Faye or Diao played things might have been different. Anyway, the point about Whelan is that he did the worst ever...what was it?...a cross? a shot? He took a corner, the ball came back to him level with the area and he just booted it straight ahead. It went out for a throw-in level with the box on the other side of the pitch - cue mass uproar of laughter from the Rams fans. I can only compare it to a school playground where an older kid spitefully whacks the ball in the direction of maximum inconvenience. (I presume he was trying to use the outside of his foot but caught it with laces).

(Whelan became a regular for Stoke soon after as Stoke zoomed up the Premier League table!)

Second point- Stoke goalie Steve Simonsen must be the only person in history to go to the barbers and ask for "a Roy Carroll please mate".

December 8th

Strange happenings on Facebook last week. Simon received a message from a bloke saying "did I work with you at Rushcliffe power station 18 years ago?" Simon pointed out that no one had shovelled coal at that age (i.e. Simon's age minus 18) since Dickens's self-explanatory *Hard Times*. Intrigued nonetheless, Simon had a look to see if there any were mutual acquaintances. What he found was page upon page of mostly South European and Middle Eastern men, most of whom were bearing their torso. In the name of research, Simon scrolled down five pages and stumbled across a "Michael Johnson of Nottingham". I've seen it with my own eyes and it is definitely *yer actual* (not the Man City midfielder or American sprinter- the other one).

What's the point of this story? Jonno's on Facebook if you want to befriend him.

December 9th

I've got out the habit of reading the Neil Hallam column recently. He seemed to have adopted the more conservative house style of the Telegraph and lost the edge of controversy that made him worth reading. Like him or not, he was always good for a few insider facts or just slating someone.

I had a few spare minutes at lunch yesterday so decided to have a look what I'd missed. Hallam was back on form, saying he thought Phil Brown was "a poser and a clot" (in his Derby days) before referring to his "lavishly Tangoed features". Great, Neil Hallam doing what he does best. The column was dated November 27th. I scrolled up and there was no column for last week. I looked at the columnists photo's on the left - he was gone. Was this his parting shot or is he just on holiday? Maybe we'll find out on Thursday.

December 10th

Email received today entitled "Other Rams On Facebook":

Dean Leacock (will accept anyone and you get regular updates on his injury e.g. 'Dean is still well injured innit' as a status update).

Nacar Barazite (might want to be a bit more careful who he accepts as friends if he is to keep on joining groups called 'Fuck Stuart Atwell'* and 'Big boobs are ALWAYS in fashion')

*The controversial referee who denied us the winning goal against Forest. Earlier in the season, the same referee had awarded a goal in the Watford v. Reading match when the ball had in fact gone out for a goal-kick. Surely unprecedented?

Barnes and Tanga are on there but unwilling to accept stalker-esque friend requests.

Dickinson is also on there. His profile pic is him posing in a Borat style 'man-kini'. Maybe that's what's pissed off Jagger.

Thanks for sending us this, I enjoyed it and don't even have a Facebook account.

December 12th

A few updates on previous entries this week:

Facebook mania continues as one of the other Rams forums picked up on the December 10th entry and our hits went through the roof. The Facebook entry was one of the few things ever on the Journals not written by me - and got the biggest response. Maybe there's a hint there somewhere?

Simon has now unearthed Albrechtsen and Bisgaard on Facebook - he didn't say if he had to wade through five pages of semi-naked men to find them this time. By Monday I expect to be hearing "Trevor Hebbard's on there" or "Gary Micklewhite - is currently driving his taxi" (Please note- if you've arrived at this site by typing "naked", "men", and "semi" into Google- you're probably in the wrong place).

It seems like I was very late on the Neil Hallam news, I immediately got a couple of texts saying "didn't you know". Apparently, he's been banned from Pride Park* and subsequently axed from the Derby Telegraph. Ironic as I was thinking how conservative he'd become.

*I think "had his press privileges removed" rather than "banned" was more accurate.

December 16th

I experienced a bit of deja vu today - it was roughly a year ago when everyone was talking about Paul Ince becoming the new Rams manager. As soon as the news broke today *(Paul Ince was sacked as Blackburn manager)*, the texts and questions started: "next stop Pride Park eh?". Just to prove the efficiency of global communications, the first news came from Watford fan Big Nick in Russia. My reaction was that I'd rather go for Roberto Di Matteo as at least he seems to be on the way up. (In case you missed it, Di Matteo took over from P'Ince at MK Dons and now has them in the frame for promotion from League One). Although, it could follow a worrying trend: Martin Allen does quite well at MK Dons, gets a job above his station (Leicester) and completely bombed. P'Ince does slightly better at MK Dons, gets a job above his station and once again, completely bombed. Roberto Di Matteo does *even better* at MK Dons and then what? *(Roberto Di Matteo was appointed as West Bromwich Albion manager in July 2009)*.

(I must admit I did have a flutter on Blackburn to go down in the summer when P'ince was lining up Keith Andrews and Robbie Fowler to replace David Bentley. They were 12/1 at the time).

All this talk is a bit premature with Jagger still at the helm and with a fresh vote of confidence. However, the problem for me is not just losing but that the games are becoming increasingly boring. The brand of football we were promised hasn't materialised, despite a flicker against Sheffield Wednesday.

I can say no more than that a good friend of mine who has had real problems sleeping recently actually nodded off during the Palace game. A proper elbow-slipping-off-the knee moment when he woke up. They were amazed in the club shop when he turned up at 9am on the Monday asking when the DVD was out (the second bit isn't true but the rest is).

December 18th

The Hull Fan At Work gave me an article on Phil Brown yesterday from the Times website, which basically talked about Phil Brown being an all round good bloke, or in the journalists words "all charm, no smarm". The article was chockfull of such cheesy couplets and some of the worst puns I've ever come across. The article mentions that Phil Brown used to have a restaurant towards the end of his career (Brown's Brassiere) - about which the writer says "Trying to climb the table by day, arranging tables by night" before following it with "Brown could probably eat out free across East Yorkshire...[To] the Premier Leagues familiar ingredients, Hull have added a fresh taste, an unexpected flavour" before finishing off with "From master of the house to king of a city...Brown knows that the customers need to be satisfied just the same". No, Stop! Managing a football club is not like running a restaurant! (Not that I've done either). This was actually from a Times journalist as well, not a chancer like us.

On the subject of Hull, Phil Brown and journalists; I was telling The Hull Fan At Work about Neil Hallam slating Phil Brown (Journals December 12th) and then about Hallam having his press privileges removed at Pride Park (note to any journalist - music or football - who finds themselves without a press pass: buy a ticket you parasite). Apparently the Hull Daily Mail were banned from the KC Stadium during the Adam Pearson era. No wonder others stick to a "results and injuries" service.

December 19th

Another one from the Hull Fan At Work - he pointed me in the direction of ex-referee Jeff Winters website (pompously titled "Jeff Winter Entertainment and Media"). One of the features on the site is "Jeff's League of Injustice" where Winter analyses the weekends contentious decisions before producing a revised league table based on what the results would have been.

I think the Hull fan likes it because it puts the Tigers firmly above Arsenal and in a European place. It also makes my Blackburn bet look even better.

Unfortunately, I can't find anywhere that says we would have stayed up last season if it wasn't for those dastardly refs.

December 22nd

(Excuse the swearing in the following entry but it wouldn't work without it)
I was at a Christmas do at the weekend and heard one of the best bits of football punditry for a while. I got talking to someone and the conversation turned to Claude Davis and how Davis had managed to command a multi-million pound fee in successive transfers. Billy Davies has dropped more than a few clangers in the transfer market but my new pal was completely bemused as to why a seasoned campaigner like Neil Warnock would make such a signing. As he thoughtfully sipped his pint, he said "the thing with Neil Warnock is, he is a cunt but he's not a wanker".

The difference may be a subtle one but either word would describe the bloke sat behind me last Saturday. I know Gary Teale is not a fans favourite at the moment but the way this bloke goes on is almost obsessive - as though he's shown Teale some unrequited love and is now seeking revenge. A routine comment will be: "Teale's nowhere near his man!" when play is in our left-back position and Teale and his marker will be standing a few yards apart near the half-way line. The ultimate one though came after Ellington scuffed his volley wide in front of an open goal against Watford - the shout from behind was: "is Teale black or something!"

December 23rd

We've had an unprecedented amount of correspondence recently so it could be a readers takeover week - brilliant, I can take a rest and have some mulled wine.

First up is our newly appointed London correspondent (to avoid tax on your wages, I've got some Woolies vouchers for you mate - valid from 1st Jan).

Apparently the J-Mac PR machine is working over-time down there in the South *(McEveley was now on loan at Charlton)*. There's no shortage of big football personalities in London with five Premier League clubs, half the Big Four and tonnes of bling. You wouldn't have thought an injured, on loan, bottom-of-the-league Championship full-back would garner much interest, would you? Wrong. Apparently, last week the Metro lead with headline "Jay says Charlton are too good for the drop", this followed on from a previous J-Mac interview that even overshadowed the Spurs report! Well, if anyone knows about relegation, Jay does. There's no point asking Alan Shearer is there?

(Charlton subsequently finished bottom of the Championship, relegated with weeks to spare; whilst Alan Shearer probably does know a lot about relegation now!)

December 27th

As promised, a couple of bits from readers; both in reference to the December 22nd entry. Firstly, one reader reminds me that Neil Warnock is in fact a "wanker" - Neil Warnock is an anagram of Colin Wanker and in some football circles he is referred to simply as "Colin".

Secondly is an email from a reader who has befriended a relation of Claude Davis' agent. An odd link but a good one. A lot of Rams fans were surprised at the fee we paid for Claude - a defender signed by Sheffield United for around £2.5m but was never a regular in a relegated side. Claude's stock had somehow increased and the Rams paid £3m. Our insider claims that Clod and his agent were equally surprised. I can just imagine the Rams negotiator offering £2m - when this is met with stunned silence he adds "go on then £3m but that's our final offer".

(I've just had a look on Wikipedia for the exact fees; it says Sheff Utd. signed him for £35m and the Rams paid £50m - that's where the parachute payment went then).

The story continues that the man not known as the Caribbean Koeman isn't the brightest chap. His agent doesn't seem to be suffering though, he's off to New York and Sydney for his festive jollies - let's just hope it's not a working holiday. We don't want him banging on Jagger's door in January "Hey Paul, I've found some more glorious Yanks and Aussies for you".

December 29th

After yesterdays defeat by Ipswich, it was no massive surprise to hear that Jagger had gone. It wasn't the worst performance but the general mood afterwards seemed to be "enough is enough". Some fans in the East Stand were singing "Jewell Out", whilst others were wandering home with plenty of time on the clock - no hope and no reason for optimism. Every conversation I heard on the way out was on the same theme - it's not working and something has to change. We will never know if Jagger would turn the corner so he will go down in history, fairly or not, as one of the clubs worst ever managers.

I was reading a post-defeat interview with Jewell a couple of weeks ago when he was saying his usual "I've done it in this division before and I'll do it again given time". By coincidence, I also read an interview with George Burley about dropping Kris Boyd from the Scotland squad. His reasoning was something like "I'm only interested in current form, if I was going on past achievements, Kenny Dalglish would be playing up front for Scotland". You could apply Burley's logic to Jagger's situation.

It was fitting that it should happen against Ipswich who were themselves waving "Magilton Out" banners; not because Ipswich are particularly awful but because they have gone completely stale. The fact that they have doubled us in little over a month tells a story. (Ipswich fans may have a point. Of their 16 man squad yesterday, a quarter of them were ex-Ipswich players re-signed by Magilton after proving elsewhere to be officially *not that good*. For the record: Wright, Miller, Counago and Ambrose. Talk about going backwards!).

I got a text from Big Nick quite early on today where he suggested Aidy Boothroyd (Nick's a Watford fan). I jokingly said we'd probably have Chris Hutchings for six months as he and Jagger seem to have a pact - Jagger leaves, Hutchings takes over, Hutchings gets sacked (see Bradford and Wigan). A few hours later I logged onto the Telegraph website "Hutchings is early favourite to become permanent Derby County Manager". Other people available include Stan Ternent, Colin Calderwood and Billy Davies. And of course P'Ince.

Jewell's Legacy

There is no doubt that Paul Jewell took on one of the biggest challenges anyone could face in football when he became Rams manager in November 2007. There is also no doubt that statistically, Jewell will be remembered as one of the worst managers in footballing history.

Although sharing the 2007/8 season with Billy Davies, unfortunately for Jewell, it was he who finally took us down with the lowest ever points total in the top flight. Jewell was far from blameless though, he failed to win a single Premier League fixture.

One thing Paul Jewell did do whilst Derby County manager, was sign an astonishing amount of players: eight during January 2008, followed by another fourteen by the end of August. Despite adding to this with further loan deals and Luke Varney, Jewell could never find the winning combination. Jewell could be forgiven for his January '08 signings because of the dire situation the Rams were in; who would want to join us? Unfortunately his propensity for taking a gamble (e.g. Villa and Sterjovski) continued as players such as Kazmierczak, Zadkovich, Dickinson and Pereplotkins only served to swell a squad already bloated by Billy Davies' jetsam and flotsam. At the time of writing, many of Jewell's signings are already heading for the exit door. Ironically, one of the few Jewell signings who looks to have a future is Robbie Savage; a player completely written off by Jewell.

Jewell often endeared himself to both the press and fans with his self-depreciating banter and most Rams fans hold no ill-will towards "Jagger" despite his disastrous tenure. I'm sure he would be welcome back at Pride Park any time to make the half-time prize draw...just don't let him near the dug-out.

"How's your match fitness lads?"

David Lowe discovers Andy Todd and Mo Camara days before for the Carling Cup Semi-final versus Manchester United.

PART 3

"It was heartwrenching to leave...but if there's one club to leave for, it was here."

Nigel Clough January 2009

If ever there was an occasion to use the cliché "a week's a long time in football", then it would be in relation to the events that took place between 3 -10 January 2009. Let us recap:

January 3rd: The Rams play non-league Forest Green away in the FA Cup with Chris Hutchings as caretaker manager. Robbie Savage, Mo Camara, Giles Barnes and Liam Dickinson are all recalled to the squad. Despite being 0-2 and 2-3 behind, the Rams win 4-3 courtesy of a late penalty.

January 4th: The Rams are drawn against Nottingham Forest in the 4th round of the FA Cup. In contrast to the league game two months ago, Forest are now buoyant after a 0-2 FA Cup win at Man City. The Rams are managerless but Forest now have a replacement for the sacked Colin Calderwood...ex-Rams boss Billy Davies.

January 6th: Nigel Clough is appointed as the new Derby County manager. After years of speculation linking him with both Derby and Forest, Clough ends ten years at Burton Albion to join his hometown club. Clough will officially take charge over the forthcoming days. However, temporary boss Chris Hutchings leaves the club with immediate effect leaving Academy coach David Lowe to take charge for the Carling Cup semi-final first leg at home to Manchester United. The Rams' third manager in barely a week, with a fourth waiting in the wings.

January 7th: David Lowe takes charge for his one and only game as Derby County manager. His task? To take a team who have struggled past non-league opposition only four days earlier and try to beat the current English, European and World Champions. No problem.

Lowe began by shocking everyone and picking Andy Todd, the first time Todd had even been in the squad this season. Lowe gave Mo Camara his second home start in two years and Mile Sterjovski started for the first time this season.

Lowe also makes two decisions that will benefit the Rams for the remainder of the campaign. Firstly, he played Kris Commons as a "second striker" behind Rob Hulse. Commons had thus far been frustratingly erratic on the wing but he had an outstanding match versus United and would remain in the middle for the rest of the season. Commons' improvement was so dramatic that the press would regular link him with a move to the Premier League. Secondly, David Lowe reintroduced Robbie Savage to the Rams fans. Savage didn't take the field until the 87th minute and barely had time to contribute. Under Jewell, Savage's popularity was at an all-time low. However, swept along in the euphoria of the night, it was impossible not to see Savage as part of something infinitely better than we had a fortnight ago.

The Rams won 1-0 thanks to a Kris Commons goal. It was played down by United fans as being their reserves or youth team, so its worth remembering that eight of the players involved on that night were also involved in the European Cup final of 2009.

January 8th: Nigel Clough officially takes charge of Derby County. He announces that he will be joined by ex-Rams Andy Garner and Martin Taylor along with former Forest winger Gary Crosby. All three join from Burton Albion leaving new Burton manager Roy McFarland with only the physio remaining of the backroom staff.

January 10th: The rollercoaster week comes to end as Nigel's first scheduled match in charge – Cardiff away – is postponed due to bad weather.

Nigel Clough's first game in charge came on January 17th at home to QPR. If ever a match justified the common phrase of new managers – "there's a lot of work to do" – this was it. A 0-2 defeat. Clough's second match was, on paper, slightly more challenging than QPR at home. On 20th January The Rams travelled to Old Trafford to defend a 1-0 lead in the second leg of the Caring Cup semi-final. Despite going 0-3 down after 34 minutes, The Rams emerged from the match with some pride and confidence after eventually losing 4-2. Robbie Savage came on as a half-time substitute and changed the whole tempo of the game. He was to remain a fixture in the team for the remainder of the season. Giles Barnes also made his first significant contribution since returning from injury by scoring twice; once from a penalty and once from a free kick despite being on the field for only twenty minutes.

The action continued relentlessly and only three days later, The Rams were at home to Forest in the FA Cup. Much of the pre-match build-up focussed on the two managers. Clough would be facing Forest for the first time as Rams manager whilst Forest were now managed by Billy Davies. In the event, the game was an anti-climax. Despite taking an early lead, Derby failed to finish the job and, almost predictably, Robert Earnshaw equalised in front of the travelling fans – complete with somersault. Just to cap the disappointment, the fifth round draw was made days later and paired the winners with Manchester United. To play United in the Carling Cup was a pleasant distraction; to play them in both cups was an odds-on defeat without the novelty.

On Wednesday the fourth of February, Derby travelled to the City Ground for the FA Cup replay. Again, the press played up the rivalry and reminded everyone how long ago it was since the Rams had beaten Forest away (28 years).

To the Rams horror, Forest raced into a two goal lead within 14 minutes. Thankfully, Rob Hulse managed to pull a goal back before half-time. Derby stepped up a gear in the second half with a display of attacking football that Forest could not cope with. Paul Green equalised before Kris Commons' deflected long range shot proved to be the winner. Commons had looked nervous when facing his ex-club in November and had then missed the home cup tie. Returning to the City Ground, Commons had been shocked at the level of abuse he had received from Forest fans early in the match. He soon shed any inhibitions he may have had and ran Forest ragged in a 3-2 Rams victory.

The FA Cup run came to an end with a 1-4 home defeat by Manchester United. Perhaps United had been surprised by Derby's resilience in the Carling Cup or maybe they just didn't want a replay. Whatever the reasoning, the United starting line up included Ferdinand, Giggs and Ronaldo (amongst others) and was significantly stronger than the team eventually defeated by Everton in the FA Cup semi-final. Despite being defeated in both cups by United, it should be remembered that The Rams scored four times against United in a near three month period when the Reds conceded only one other goal against an English club.

The final instalment in this breathless period came on February 21st as the Rams took on Forest once more at the City Ground, this time in the league. On this occasion it was the Rams who scored the early goal through Lewin Nyatanga after five minutes. The Rams extended the lead through Rob Hulse in the second half before Steve Davies made it safe from the penalty spot with over twenty minutes still remaining. It was such a commanding lead that Forest fans streamed out of the stadium and many missed Earnshaw's late consolation goal against 10 man Rams (McEveley had come off injured after all subs had been used). When the Forest DJ played celebratory music for the goal, it was Rams fans who danced ironically.

Off the park

Amidst all the excitement on the pitch, Clough had also begun tinkering with his squad. Adam Pearson had already said that Varney's signing was the January kitty so the emphasis was on Clough to move some players out with little room for incomers.

Clough allowed Claude Davis to join Crystal Palace on loan and on the eve of the transfer deadline, Giles Barnes joined Premier League Fulham on loan. Barnes was barely fit after a long term injury, so it made sense all round for the Rams to collect a significant loan fee for a player who could take at least another month to be firing again. Barnes had expressed his desire to move to the Premier League so the transfer would become permanent if he proved himself at that level. Four years after his debut, it was still not entirely clear what Giles Barnes' strongest position was; neither a winger nor a striker, he was often considered too attack-minded to play central midfield. Hampered by injury, he had done little for The Rams since the promotion season.

Incoming was Motherwell striker Chris Porter for £400,000. Clough said he wanted a striker who was currently scoring goals and in one statement summed up Jewell's signings in that department. Although Jewell had spent heavily on our strike force (approximately £7m) all the signings had one thing common – they all needed to be improved. Hulse because of injury; Ellington after a horrid season at Watford; Villa in a new country; Dickinson at a new level; and Varney out of form. Only Hulse had looked a success and all expectation was on him.

Aside from the new signings, Clough also breathed life into three players who were all but written off under Jewell – Savage, Teale and McEveley. Savage's renaissance has been well documented but equally as surprising was the turnaround in Gary Teale's fortunes. Derby fans are usually a tolerant bunch but Gary Teale is one of the few players I can say has regularly taken some stick from the fans. With Commons now used in a central role, Teale was switched to left-wing, a role he'd occasionally played with little success under both Davies and Jewell. This also coincided with an emphasis from Clough to get the ball wide and get crosses in. Teale did the simple things very effectively and his confidence grew. Teale had been in and out of the matchday 16 under previous managers and sent out on loan. Clough gave Teale a regular starting berth. With more security and increased confidence, Teale began to thrive and became a regular supply-line for Rob Hulse.

Jay McEveley, like Teale, had also been a player greeted with a groan by some fans (myself included) and had also been loaned out by Jewell with seemingly no future at the club. However, Clough quite evidently preferred McEveley to Jordan Stewart and like Teale, Jay rewarded Clough for his faith with some more assured displays.

On the park

In the background of The Rams' high profile cup matches, Derby's league form was steadily improving with a movement towards attacking football. Clough recorded his first league victory on January 31st in a 2-1 home victory against Coventry, a scoreline which flattered the visitors who had five shots compared to Derby's twenty. The winning run continued as Derby beat Plymouth and Blackpool, scoring seven goals in the process, and culminated in the 3-1 win at the City Ground. Derby's fourth straight league victory.

The run was to end on 27th February when The Rams lost 1-2 at Doncaster. The match was notable only for Robbie Savage's first goal for the club – a curling free-kick which was bizarrely shortlisted in the top 10 Rams goals ever on the official club website. The defeat at Doncaster signalled the end of a heady period for Rams fans which had seen us play Forest and Manchester United each three times in a period of less than six weeks, not to mention the second coming of Clough. There seemed to be a collective exhalation of breath after the Doncaster defeat that said "back to reality".

Rams players give their verdict on Robert Earnshaw's somersault, following his consolation goal in Derby's victory at the City Ground.

Journals of Derventio – post-Jewell to February

December 30th

Is there anyone who *hasn't* been linked with the Rams job yet? I said a couple of weeks ago (Journals December 16th, exactly two weeks ago) about getting Roberto Di Matteo. The MK Dons chairman is obviously an avid reader of the Journals - I read today that Di Matteo has been tied up with a two-year extension to his contract.

Simon is in Sydney at the moment (no he's not Claude Davis' agent- Journals Dec 27th) but he texted me this morning just to remind me that he predicted almost a year ago that Jagger would be "Gregory all over again".

Whilst in Sydney, Simon has had the misfortune to find himself surrounded by backpackers. He got asked the typically banal backpacker question of "have you ever travelled?". Simon replied "No, I popped out for a paper in Ilkeston three weeks ago and now I'm lost". Well, if you ask a stupid question...

January 3rd

A bit of Eastern European transfer spec from Big Nick:
"Local transfer rumour here [he's in Hungary] Savage coming to Budapest. To join Bobby Davison at Fradi"
I asked him who "Fradi" were and what Bobby Davison was doing there. Now for the bizarre bit:
"He is manager. It's Ferencvaros. They are owned by Sheffield United chairman now".

For those less au fait with Hungarian football, Ferencvaros are arguably the biggest club in Hungary and no strangers to the Champions League. How did that happen? Last I heard of Bobby Davison, he had a bbc coaching job somewhere (that's bibs, balls and cones not broadcasting). Another ex-Ram to link to our current vacancy maybe?

(I've just checked the ever reliable wikipedia. For BD's managerial career it has "2000 Guiseley, 2008 Ferencvaros")

January 4th

(Written after the FA Cup 4th round paired us with Forest)
Surely there's a trivia question waiting to happen about playing Forest in consecutive rounds of the FA Cup. I just saw an old stager on Sky News, possibly John McGovern, who said it was a "fairy tale draw for both clubs". A fairy tale? Out-of-form managerless Rams versus bang-in-form Red Dogs under Billy Davies: ghost story more like. I'd have happily taken Kettering.

I had a social engagement pencilled in for that day, after lengthy discussions I compromised with "ok, we'll go for the 24th but don't confirm yet in case we draw Forest or something stupid". My brother is less fortunate, he has an anniversary trip to Paris booked. The current deal on the table for him is to go to the Forest game at the cost of cancelled flights and a more expensive trip at a later date.

At least if Forest start their "worst club in history" chants again, we can respond with "worst boss in history" - I'm sure 30,000 voices will drown out Davies' shouts of "hang on, at least I won *one*".

Ferencvaros news tomorrow...

January 5th

It appears that Ferencvaros aren't quite the European giants of yesteryear anymore (see Journals Jan 3rd). No sooner had I written Saturday's piece than we received an email to tell us that Craig Short is also there. Once I scratched the surface (via Wikipedia and Big Nick), it soon became apparent that "Fradi" are now in the second tier of Hungarian football after being relegated due to financial problems a couple of years ago. Sheffield United took them over and installed board member Terry Robinson as chairman (Robinson was Stan Ternent's chairman at Bury and features frequently in Stan's book).

The Craig Short link is a strange one, I saw in the Observer last year (also on Sky Sports apparently) that he had a sailing business in the Lake District. The first question was:

So you retired once and were tempted out of it. Any chance of it happening again?
"No. I'm happy sailing, thanks. I shouldn't really have been tempted back last time, either - I wish I'd stuck to my guns".

When I first got wind of the credit crunch I immediately thought "those sailing lessons on Lake Windmere with a large headed ex-Scarbrough player are going to have to go", I can only think others thought the same. I think the clue to why Craig is now in the Hungarian second division is in a later question: Q."What does the business involve?" A. "It's mainly corporate stuff". Woolies management away days? Zavvi's Christmas do?

If you wanted yet further confirmation that Ferencvaros aren't what they used to be, they also have 35 year old ex-Chesterfield (and Sheff Utd.) Paul Shaw playing for them. Shaw was bald when playing for Millwall in his early 20's - he must be running round with a skeleton's head nowadays.

(Big Nick advised me to look on the official website www.ftc.hu thanks Nick, its all in Hungarian. Multi-lingual people can't help showing off can they? He also failed to warn me that the welcome page automatically plays the club anthem - to the tune of YMCA!)

January 6th

(The following entry refers to Nigel Clough's appointment as Rams boss)
I think Adam Pearson let the cat out the bag on the Clough story a couple of days ago. Not with his straight-bat responses to direct questioning but when he started saying "it's not him" when asked about others. As soon as chairmen (or managers) start ruling people out, journalists soon see who's left.

One of the Clough stories I read today contained probably the best piece of spin I've ever seen from Adam Pearson. Talking about The Rams' rumoured shortlist of two non-league managers, a coach and a League One novice*, Pearson said something like "[the candidates] aren't overburdened specifically with Championship experience". It was on the Telegraph website earlier but has now been superseded by news of the appointment. Can you imagine: "what experience do you have of being a pilot Mr. Smith?", "well, I'm not overburdened by experience of specifically flying aeroplanes", "fine, the jobs yours".

The phrase immediately entered the vocabulary at work, usage this afternoon included "can the new employee drive?","no, she's not overburdened with car ownership" and "how are we doing with this contract?", "well, we're not overburdened with clients". The Hull Fan At Work pledged to say it in a meeting we had that afternoon but he was gazumped by a colleague who I think said it un-ironically after his subconscious was bombarded by overuse in the afternoon.

For the record, as if it matters, I'm quite pleased with the appointment of Clough. It's definitely given me more enthusiasm for the cup tie with those dastardly Dogs and Silly Davies, I'm completely hyped up now!

On the subject of the FA Cup, a reader from Surrey sent me an account of Saturdays game. The beginning really emphasises the difference between playing Forest Green and Manchester United:
"As my ticket allowed me access to Forest Green's Premier Club (a lounge where you could get a beer), I accessed the stand through a door which was situated directly next to the visiting directors seats. It's only when I paused to put my

scarf on as I emerged for the second half, that I realised that I was standing 4 seats away from a reasonably glum looking Adam Pearson - and that's when we'd managed to level the game. It is to my shame and regret that I didn't shuffle over and press my case for him to put an international call in to Igor Stimac to take over the reins. Had we still been two nil down I might have had the balls to do so."

*The short-list was supposedly - Nigel Clough, Dean Saunders, Chris Hutchings and Darren Ferguson.

January 8th

(Written after the Carling Cup victory against Manchester United)
I don't know where to start with the Man U game so I'll probably write a lengthier piece for the Times column so it reaches a wider audience i.e. Man Utd. fans. Where do you begin? Well, for starters, hats off to David Lowe. He has one game in charge with no prospect of getting the job. Instead of just sending out Saturday's team again, he makes the jaw-dropping selections of Todd and Sterjovski and tweaks the formation - bingo! The European Champions are defeated.

David Lowe, like Chris Hutchings, is also a Jagger man so it makes you wonder what kind of conversations they had about players. Hutchings immediately made five changes for Saturday (some forced), then Lowe shuffles the pack yet again. Jewell favourites Kaz and Zadkovich are nowhere to be seen despite being allowed extra subs, whilst Camara, Todd, Sterjovski, Dicko and Sav are all back on the scene.

Anyway, we don't get many chances to be happy, so let's enjoy this while it lasts. Regardless of the second leg, last night I felt proud to be a Derby fan once more. The Rams were immense and for one night only, Man Utd. were made to look truly Man Ure.

January 9th

I'll save the Times column until Sunday as not overwrite the current one too soon. In the meantime a couple more observations about Wednesday's game which probably won't make it in:

1) It's a shame that a lot of people will miss out on the memento of a free programme from Wednesday's match (myself included). In theory a nice gesture by the club; in practice an organisational shambles. The normal programme sellers were taken off-post and as I walked my normal route to the ground (which passes three sides), there were no free programmes to be seen. As I walked past the back of the East Stand a recorded message was being looped every few seconds: "Derby County fans - please collect your free scarf and programme before entering the stadium". "Where from?" I thought. As I approached the club shop to meet the Jackal, there was the answer - a huge man-tangle* resembling an aid drop in Darfur.

2) We saw Colin Todd at the Ice Rink on Derby Market Place last Saturday. Chris started chatting to him and Todd Snr. confirmed Andy was still alive, fully fit and "just bored really, he wants to play". As if by magic, three days later the Renaissance Man appears. Anyone seen Pereplotkins' old man?

*A phrase not used for ages but has enjoyed a comeback since its liberal use in Bad Worse Worst. I knew my Dad had actually read the book when he jumped on me and my son and said "let's have a man-hug, no I mean a man-tangle".

The following was written for the Times on-line. When written, it received a couple of comments contesting some of the facts. Firstly someone wrote that the game had sold-out but the lower crowd was due to segregation issues. I would dispute this as Pride Park has sold-out many times with a large away following and this has not caused the stadium to be 10% below capacity. The second point was that Man Utd. actually had 5,000 and not 7,000 tickets. This may well be correct as my 7,000 was purely what I had been told by a colleague.

They didn't come to see United

Last Wednesday, Derby County played in their first major semi-final for over thirty years against a club currently crowned English, European and World Champions. The big headline was that the Rams were victorious by a single goal in the first of two legs. An equally curious statistic was that the crowd was 30,194, 3,000 less than capacity. Given that Man Utd. brought 7,000 fans, the match was watched by less Rams fans than the average Championship match. So why would Derby fans rather see Doncaster than Man Utd?

I think the answer has to be a combination of factors. The first one being that the Rams are more likely to beat Doncaster than Man Utd. (although actual results were contrary to this theory). The game was two-legged so even in the event of a Derby victory, the chances of reaching Wembley are only slightly increased. Rams fans are a loyal bunch whose main interest is seeing our own club, not the opposition. Having said that, Derby, like most towns and cities, is home to a lot of United fans who "have always supported them but can never get a ticket". Well, tickets were available but the Sky habit is hard to break. Ticket prices were reasonable (my seat was £29.50 compared with £44 for the league fixture last season) but the sub-zero temperatures make you realise why the phrase "fair weather supporters" was invented.

Another factor could be the Carling Cup stigma of teams playing reserves and kids. True, United did field many players not good enough for a regular first team berth but some cost up to £18m. Almost all were internationals with Tevez, Vidic and Scholes being joined later on by Ronaldo, Rooney and Carrck. In the interests of fairness, The Rams also fielded several reserves with Camara, Todd and Sterjovski being given their first Pride Park starts of the season.

For those who didn't see the match, United were, by Fergie's own admission, well below par. Roy Carroll didn't have a shot to save whilst Derby squandered chances to win by a greater margin. We're under no illusions though; as Ferguson said, Man U. would fancy their chances at home against anyone and I think that sums it up.

Anyway, this is a Derby County column so enough about United and more about The Rams. Since Jewell's departure, Derby have played two and won two under two different caretaker managers (Chris Hutchings and David Lowe). Both managers selected dramatically different squads to Jewell's, including the likes of Savage, Camara, Sterjovski, Todd and Dickinson; a group who had barely featured under Jewell this season. There were always rumours of dressing room rifts under Jewell and this certainly suggests some players were not in the "in-crowd".

A couple of months ago I wrote in this column about the disappearance of Andy Todd after we signed an unfit aged centre half (Darren Powell) and continued to ignore our own fully fit aged centre half. Todd's dominance of Tevez on Wednesday leaves Rams fans even more puzzled to Todd's alienation by Jewell.

Mo Camara is another interesting case. This was only his second Pride Park start in two years (the other also being in the Carling Cup last season). Admittedly, Camara always looks on the verge of catastrophe but rarely actually makes the fatal error. Contrast this with Jay McEveley who looks a decent player for 85 minutes of most matches but generally does make the fatal error. Derby's record with Camara playing is quite amazing - his last run in the first team under Billy Davies yielded eight straight league victories - so we signed McEveley. Now

Mo's back with two wins in two including a clean sheet against the English (etc.) Champions; and half an hour against arguably the best player in the world. Jordan Stewart's suspension ends soon though so we might not see Mo again for a while.

If any non-Derby fan is still reading this, we're not getting carried away. A result at Old Trafford is still required but let's enjoy the moment while we can. With (yet another) new era beginning at Derby, it's not a bad way to start.

January 12th

Billy Davies is a man of many talents; two of which are rubbing people up the wrong way and putting a dampener on impressive victories. By way of introduction to the Forest players and fans, he said the following after Saturday's away victory at fellow relegation candidates Charlton:
"...we showed our age in the first twenty minutes. Physically it was men against boys...the younger boys have to grow up fast and we need to bring in some older lads. When I looked at the bench with 20 minutes to go I saw a couple of babies next to me".

By my reckoning Billy Davies hasn't made a good signing since August 2006 (with the exception of David Jones) so lets hope his team rebuilding is well under way by the 23rd. One rumour is that he is trying to sign Claude Davis. Often, if the buying and selling club meet soon after, it's agreed that the transferred player won't participate. If Claude signs for Forest, it should be part of the deal that he *must play* in the Cup tie.

January 14th

Some quiz questions for a future generation:
1) Which team played a "Forest" in consecutive rounds of the FA Cup?
2) Which team had four different managers in four consecutive matches?

3) Which team won more matches against Premier League teams when outside the division than in it?

And January is barely halfway through! It should be a good year.

A farewell to Andrejs Pereplotkins written for Ramspace after his season loan was cancelled by mutual consent:

Andrejs Pereplotkins Aug 2008 – Jan 2009

Pereplotkins arrived on trial a week before the season began and played the first two matches before disappearing for ever. The whole episode suggested we were not as prepared for the season as Jewell and Pearson had suggested.

Epitaph

An early assessment of "Candido Costa-ski" proved to be bang on.

January 18th

(Written after the home defeat to QPR)
I did the Observer Fans Verdict for only the second time this season yesterday and got massively misquoted. The first error was when the journo quoted me as saying "...Forest at home next Saturday", enough to sow the seeds of "this bloke doesn't know what he's talking about" *(The Forest game would be on a Friday)*. Worse was to come though; in the "Who played well and who had a nightmare?" section I was quoted as saying "Collectively we were poor. Luke Varney did OK". I just spoke to Simon who assured me that people would just think I was joking but if you didn't go to the game, you probably wouldn't see the error. For the record, Varney was poor, gave the ball away initially for both goals, never looked like scoring and was hauled off before the hour mark. How this translated as "Varney did OK" I'll never know.

Onto a completely different subject, when scanning the line-ups this morning I noticed a "Kazimierczak" on the bench for Darlington. Now, Kaz has disappeared without trace since Jagger's departure but surely it couldn't be him? I had a look on the net and found "Przemyslaw Kazimierczak, 6' 4" born in Poland". How many people in British football could fit this description? Well, apparently at least two. He's a young goalie on loan from Bolton. For the record, Darlo's squad no.1 is ex-Ram Andy Oakes. Przemyslaw Kazimierczak must be John Smith in Polish.

January 19th

We've two massive games this week: At Man United we have nothing to lose and everything to gain; against Forest it's the opposite, defeat would be horrendous. One game at a time though, so I'll save the Forest build up until later in the week.

The Man United game is huge but United have really done their best to be dismissive. Fergie again talked about "playing the kids" and Man U. fans seem to repeat that at every opportunity. The fact is that 3 of the back 4 at Pride Park played at Bolton *(United's previous game)*; Anderson and Tevez also played; and you can hardly call Scholes, Kuszczak and £15m Nani "kids".

I can sense a definite division of opinion amongst Rams fans: some can't wait for Tuesday; for others, Friday is the one that matters. It was interesting to read the story about ticket sales last week. The spin was that the Rams were set to break the record for an away following at Old Trafford. The fact was that only two-third's of the tickets had been sold, despite being on general sale for well over a week (season ticket holders had had since mid-December). Our away following is likely to be huge and fantastic but there hasn't been the scramble for tickets we saw for the Play-Off's. It's likely that our core following will be topped up by football tourists in the same way that Burton Albion sold 11,000 for Old Trafford.

Well, as I said, nothing to lose on Tuesday night so let's see what happens.

January 21st

(Following the Rams 2-4 defeat at Old Trafford)
At least we ended last night on a good note - if the game was five minutes longer we could even have pinched it. Extra time against 8 fit men would definitely have been interesting *(Man Utd. finished the match with several walking wounded after using all their subs)*. Now we can concentrate properly on the Forest match and I've kicked off proceedings with a new Times column.

The following is a Times on-line column written before the Forest FA Cup tie

If there's one club...

As Derby County fans prepare for the clubs biggest cup tie for several days, the build up to the Forest match is likely to focus more on off-the-field events than those on it. Both Derby and Forest have brand new managers: Forest lead by ex-Rams boss Billy Davies and Derby by – no introduction needed – Nigel Clough. When Clough announced he was leaving Burton, he said ""It was heartwrenching to leave…but if there's one club to leave for, it was here." Cries of "Ouch" could be heard all the way down the A52.

Having played over 400 games for Forest, it may seem odd to the outsider that Nigel is so attached to the Rams - and Rams fans to Nigel. My personal experiences of Nigel as a player were in the late 80's and early 90's. I went to school in a town at the exact mid-point of Derby and Nottingham; Forest were enjoying some moderate cup success and Nigel was banging the goals in, especially against Derby. I have to concede he wasn't my favorite player.

Time heals such wounds though and Nigel began his managerial career at Burton Albion. Although Burton is in Staffordshire, most Rams fans look out for Burton's results and wish them well, in the same slightly patronising way that

Forest do with Notts County. Nigel grew up playing football in the local leagues of Derbyshire and has always lived in the area. If you overlook his 84-93 blip, it's clear where his heart lies.

In the red corner we have pantomime villain Billy Davies. Again, it may seem odd to the outsider why Rams fans should dislike Billy Davies (with the possible exception of those from Preston) after his heroic promotion in 2006/7. Forest are currently in fine form under Davies with several consecutive wins but apparently they are not playing well. That was the story of our 2006/7 promotion season - not playing well and winning. Playing ugly, scrappy football and winning. To compound matters, Davies regularly made snipes at the board and fans, coupled with wildly self-congratulatory comments. We were winning though.

Once promoted, we continued to play ugly, scrappy football, Davies continued to moan and the Rams got hammered by all and sundry. Davies had no goodwill in the tank so it was a case of "good riddance". And now he turns up 16 miles down the road.

So now Davies returns to Pride Park with our most fierce rivals. Meanwhile, we are managed by a man named Clough against a team who sing about Clough week in, week out. For those who bemoan the lack of passion and sense of occasion in modern football – tune in on Friday and you might just enjoy yourself.

January 22nd

With the media gaze fixed temporarily on the East Midlands, Billy Davies has really been in his element this week. As Rams fans, we should be used to Davies' grandiose claims but I think he has surpassed himself with: "I was very confident of keeping Derby in the League. That first transfer window would always have been difficult...But I was looking forward to the second one." Maybe he could have kept us up, what's to say he wouldn't have? (Apart from our points tally when he left, his appalling run of signings from January 2007, the fact we hadn't even scored an away goal, our teams complete lack of fight and spirit...I could go on).

A reader emailed me last week just as Billy was getting into his stride with the usual "it wasn't my fault" soundbites. Apparently Davies signed-off by saying we'll all be able to read all about it in the book he's writing! At least that explains where he's been for the last year. My brother says he used a similar line after leaving Preston and it's not the only quote he's recycled. Billy has also been reminding everyone of his great achievements in the belief that the Rams fans treat him like a returning hero (he said the same before we played Preston two years ago).

I don't know whether it is tongue in cheek or not but Davies is talking as though he's going to get a genuinely good reception, conceding only that "a small minority might be negative". The Hull Fan At Work asked me last week what proportion of Rams fans would give Davies some stick - my guess was about 95%. I might be wrong though, it wouldn't be the first time I've been out of step with the zeitgeist.

January 25th

(The following entry was written after the Rams 1-1 draw at home to Forest in the FA Cup. Billy Davies was absent from the match due to his son undergoing an operation in Glasgow)
I won't be making any wisecracks about Billy Davies, as football does become "just a game" when your family are in hospital. However, much in the same way as young debutants talk about "unfortunate circumstances but I've got to take my chance", Davies' absence was to the Rams advantage. Dislike him or hate him, Billy Davies is second to none when it comes to managing Championship sides to beat other Championship sides. With us leading 1-0 at half time and a team talk from professional gardener Ned Kelly* to come, I just couldn't see us not winning.

Forest players and fans celebrated at the end like they'd won the FA Cup itself, their actions an admission that they were the underdogs who had escaped with a result; rather than equals satisfied with a draw.

Now we've got to play them twice more within a month - this is what the Scottish Premier League must feel like. (It could be worse - Blackburn and Sunderland will meet twice in the league, once in the Carling Cup and twice in the FA Cup - not teams you'd wish to see five times in a season if you didn't support them).

David "Ned" Kelly was placed on gardening leave for a whole season by Preston to prevent him joining The Rams. After only months in the job, he again found himself with time on his hands.

January 26th

The subs bench for the Forest match might provide some none-too-subtle clues to who has a future at the club. Jason Beardsley and Mitch Hanson were both included at the expense of Zadkovich, Sterjovski, Davis, Dickinson, Kazimierczak, and Camara (in addition, the Duke and J-Mac were also missing but possibly injured).

One player who was included was Tito Villa. Was it to make up the numbers, or could he stay after being an early favourite to leave this window? We received the following email from a reader about Tito last week:

"I might have cracked the Tito mystery.
I've never seen any Mexican club football before but I watched a couple of games on the sports channel while I was there and it surprised me how poor the quality was. It seemed like they were playing at the pace of a Sunday afternoon kick-about on the park, midfield getting loads of space and time on the ball, but the skill level of a mid-table League One team*. The finishing

was particularly bad, like the strikers were thinking "I know I'm going to get 30 attempts on goal in this match so I don't have to try too hard. As long as one goes in that should do it" I think Tito's selling point as "high-scoring Mexican league striker" is a bit misleading. I reckon even I could be a "high-scoring Mexican league striker" if they gave me long enough.."

Ever the spin doctor, Adam Pearson said the following regarding a return to Mexico for Villa:
"That is where he built his reputation and probably where the most fertile market for him is." I think Pearson has also "cracked the Tito mystery"

*This may explain why 4 or Tito's 6 goals this season were against League 1 opposition. Tito was indeed to return to Mexico in July 2009 with The Rams astonishingly recouping the majority of the £2m we paid for him.

January 28th

It looks like Robbie Savage will be staying for the foreseeable. A place he certainly won't be going to is the Lebanese club where he enjoyed a visit earlier in the year. According to last months World Soccer "In Lebanon - Al Ansar have parted company with Welsh coach Roy Thomas".

(Earlier in the season, it seemed Savage would definitely be on his way out if only someone would take him. One of the few expressions of interest was a Lebanese club who Robbie went to visit in November 2008).

In other news, our old pal Lionel Ainsworth is on the move again- this time signing for Huddersfield. I make this his fourth permanent club in around 18 months (The Rams, Hereford, Watford and Huddersfield). Could Lionel's career be going a bit *Marvin Robinson*? Hopefully not.

January 29th

It may appear from results that things haven't changed much since Clough's arrival. But what do the insiders think? Writing in today's Derby Telegraph, Paul Green addresses the question of "[has] there been a change to our style of play since Nigel Clough has come in?"
Green says "Paul Jewell wanted us to go forward but the new manager wants us to take the game to the opposition...". Is that a "yes" or a "no" then Greenie? In my (not too distant) day that meant exactly the same thing!

January 30th

During the 1970's when the Beach Boys' Brian Wilson was suffering from "mental health issues", he was treated by a particularly unconventional psychologist, Eugene Landy. One of Landy's theories was that people only had space in their head for one "mad" person so thought that if he started to act bizarrely, Brian Wilson would gradually become "normal". Could the same theory apply within a football club?

Two years ago we had mad-skinhead Stephen Bywater; Action Man eyes darting about; swearing on TV and generally appearing to be off his tête. Then we signed Roy Carroll. Now we have normal, sensible haircut, "steady Eddie" Stephen Bywater who has just been crowned the clubs Teen Pride Ambassador.

February 1st

Hat's off to the Pride Park DJ's for digging out Sultans of Ping's early nineties album track "Give him a ball and a yard of grass", a song written about Nigel Clough (played after Saturdays victory). Not that I particularly like the song but it's unique and relevant to the Rams whilst also being slightly obscure. The only problem is that it on Saturday it sounded like Scandinavian death metal being played on Long Wave radio*.

If anyone has a digitally re-mastered version, get it to Pride Park post-haste!

*(Or for those of who'd appreciate the comparison - it sounded like someone saying "give him a ball a yard of grass" a few times during MBV's ten minute "noise holocaust" interlude in the live version of You Made Me Realise).

February 2nd

What exactly is a good goal scoring ratio? One in two is often seen as benchmark but this is 20+ goals a season and not many people do that every year. What brought this to mind was when Clough appointed Andy Garner to the coaching staff. I was tempted to make a wisecrack about Andy Garner sorting our strikers out but didn't because: firstly it's ignorant to think that limited players can't make good coaches (hello Steve McClaren*); and secondly because Garner's record surprised me - about 1 in 3 for the Rams (20 in 58 starts) a great record for a target man who appeared and scored in the top flight for the Rams.

I was then reading a story about a Honduran striker Birmingham were signing - Carlos Costly (£500,000 for a five month loan, insert your own gag). Alex McLeish said he had "smashing pedigree…especially for the Honduran national team". His record is 6 in 22. He's no Andy Garner then. *(Costly subsequently failed to find the net in 8 appearances for the Blues).*

Finally we have Chris Porter. As soon as the story broke on the Telegraph website, someone in the "From the forums" column was saying Porter's 9 in 21 was not good enough! (My calculations say this ratio would produce 19.7 goals over 46 games). To be fair, the poster soon got pounced on.

*McClaren's credibility may not be at its peak but anyone who has coached Man U., England and The Super Rams can't be bad. It's certainly more than Gazza, Bryan Robson or Chris Waddle (for a random sample) have achieved between them. The theory is that great players are more intuitive so don't really think about the game as much as those who have to work at it. A longer discussion could be had but not here...

A farewell to Mo Camara written for Ramspace after his Derby County contact was cancelled:

Mo Camara Aug 2006 – Jan 2009

Mighty Mo is an odd case. His last run in the team saw us win eight straight league games. He was replaced by J-Mac and things went downhill. He reappeared two years later, we won two on the trot and he helped keep a clean sheet against Man U. We lost against QPR, he was poor and so were the team. He had his contract ripped up.

Epitaph

Never looked safe but you can't argue with his record.

February 3rd

A reader emailed with a feeling of deja vu after reading Billy Davies' comments of "we'll be doing all we can to strengthen this squad" and "we need to add more quality" comments after Forest's defeat at Cardiff. I have the misfortune to see the Notts Post at work on occasion and the general theme seems to be "injuries, long-term job, need better players, blah, blah, blah...if we win or draw, I'm a football genius. If we lose it's because of the reasons already detailed". Sound familiar?

Let's hope we're hearing some more excuses tomorrow night.

February 4th

(The following entry was written after Derby's epic 3-2 FA Cup victory at the City Ground)
As predicted, there's been no end of Davies' excuses since last night, not to mention several pre-excuses before the game (the best one being about considering getting Ned Kelly registered - he wasn't exactly brilliant in his heyday).

Of his post-match comments, there are several contenders for the "how can you say that?" award. The contenders are: the line about us being a Premier League team (we were comprehensively proven *not* to be a Premier League team last season and are, embarrassingly, beneath you in the league Billy); the line about how much money we've spent (our biggest summer signing was £1.7m, Forest's was £2.65m); and finally the line about us having the parachute payments - you spent it Davies! (incidentally, none of the players he spent it on featured for The Rams last night). Billy also lamented, both before and after the match, about our squad compared to theirs. If you think you've inherited a crap squad Billy, spare a thought for poor jobless Jagger.

On the subject of where the parachute payment went, I was genuinely shocked to read today that Clod's *(Claude Davis)* contract runs until summer 2011. His agent definitely earned his cut the day we signed him.

(The following is an article written for the Times on-line following the Forest victory. There's some repetition from the previous article but it does bear repeating!)

Welcome Back Billy

Derby County fans witnessed a truly rare sight last Wednesday as the Rams defeated Notts Forest at the City Ground for the first time since Brian Clough lead the Rams to victory in 1971. What was more familiar to Rams fans was the pre and post match carping of new Forest boss Billy Davies.

Before I begin, there is no doubt that when it comes to football management, Billy Davies is excellent at what he does. What he does is manages average Championship teams to beat other Championship teams. What he also does is create the impression that the odds are constantly stacked against him and anything less than a ten-nil defeat in any given game renders him a football genius.

For the recent clash, the games began before the original home tie when Davies hilariously claimed that he was confident that he'd have kept Derby in the Premier League last season had he not been sacked. Just to recap, at the time of his departure, the Rams had won once in the league and had failed to score an away goal. We then had various comments about his exit which were almost identical to those given on leaving Preston, these could be summarised as "the truth hasn't come out – but it wasn't my fault".

Obviously fearing the possibility of defeat, Davies then upped the ante before the replay by suggesting he considered registering 43 year old David Kelly because Forest had a couple of strikers unavailable (The Rams had three central defenders but got on with it). More was to come after Billy's team squandered a 2-0 lead to go crashing out of the FA Cup. Was it due to awful marking on the two headers? No. According to Davies, Derby are a Premier League side who have spent heavily with the help of a parachute payment.

Firstly, I don't think anyone would class Derby as Premier League class after last season, especially when we were (at the time) below Forest in the table. As for money; Forest's biggest summer signing was £2.65m whilst ours was £1.7m. What really grated though was the line about the parachute payment. It has been well documented that Davies himself had spent that a year early on the likes of Claude Davis, Eddie Lewis, Benny Feilhaber, Andy Todd, Kenny Miller and Robert Earnshaw. Few of those players remain at the club and none featured last Wednesday. It's no coincidence that we won.

If Billy thought our money and squad were too much to handle, it's probably for the best that Forest didn't progress to play Man Utd. in the fifth round.

So Forest fans, like Derby and Preston supporters, you will soon be familiar with Billy's wide range of reasons for things not going right. And if things go well, he won't hesitate in letting you know who masterminded it. If only Billy would add one more phrase to his repertoire – "stop me if you've heard this one before".

February 8th

Aside from the Forest victory and general renaissance of the Rams, the big news here is the inclusion of a Bad Worse Worst review in 442 magazine. To this day, I don't know how they heard about the book but a reviewer approached Chris for a copy out the blue a couple of weeks ago.

Even better news was that it was awarded 4 out of 5. Praise indeed from someone who is not a) a blood relative b) featured in the book or c) a Rams fan. Of the 15 books reviewed only three got 4 stars and none got 5, so I think I can also stake a claim for Book of the Month. So there we have it, Bad Worse Worst, officially better than "Beckham and the Conquest of America", "Leeds United and a Life in The Press Box", "We Are The Famous, The Famous Chelsea" and many more.

February 12th

I read the paper copy of the Derby Telegraph today. Tucked away at the end of one of the stories was "Claude Davis and Tyrone Mears were in the Jamaica squad for a 0-0 draw with Nigeria at Millwall". Could this be the same Tyrone Mears who said last season "I'll be honest, I'm aiming to get in the [England] squad by the end of the season."?

I had a quick search to see if he played and went to the Jamaica Observer website; the report read "Mears, who plies his trade with Olympique Marseille of France...". Further investigation suggests that Mears hasn't actually "plied his trade" for anyone since coming on as sub back in August when we beat Preston in the Carling Cup.

Jamaica, with John Barnes now at the helm, have just been knocked out the World Cup qualifiers. Mears' apparent logic of: sign for Marseille; play in the Champions League; play for England; play in the World Cup, seems to have fallen at the first hurdle. At least he's getting a game somewhere.

February 16th

There's been a lot of rumours and factual stories regarding footballers and gambling in recent years, most notably at West Ham where Matthew Etherington was loaned hundreds of thousands of pounds by the Hammers to cover a fraction of his debt (whether he was told "sign for Stoke and we'll let you off" is unconfirmed).

Simon told me there had been a gambling scandal in Australian football recently (not the version where they wear vests) and full details were revealed by World Soccer: ex- Reading and Hibs midfielder Grant Brebner ("whose gambling problems have been well documented" according to World Soccer) gained £35 from three different bets; ex-Rangers Craig Moore was, I quote "£17 to the good after two flutters"; whilst ex-Wolves Kevin Muscat - brace yourselves - "lost £25 on a single punt". Watch out Monte Carlo!

(Just to add to the triviality, none of the players mentioned were involved in any game bet on. Basically they had had a normal football coupon by the sound of it).

February 17th

It looks like the competition is really hotting up between Jordan Stewart and J-Mac, with Stewart currently in pole position. No, not for the left-back spot but for the role of club rent-a-quote. In the past few weeks we've had: "Stewart takes heart from second half display" (after the Man Utd. away defeat); "Jordan set to tackle the Blues" (Birmingham born Stewart plays against Birmingham); and "Our spirit was willing says full-back Stewart" (after the latest Man Utd. defeat). In comparison J-Mac has only managed "McEveley's hope for a fresh start rewarded by Rams".

The face-off was in today's Telegraph in a story about them both: "Friends Stewart and McEveley up for a battle for left back place". Who got the nod? It was Stewart. "Derby County defender Jordan Stewart is relishing some "healthy competition" for the left-back spot between himself and team-mate Jay McEveley". I think J-Mac needs to have a word with his agent.

February 19th

What's with the bizarre trend of discarded Forest managers bagging Premier League jobs? First we had Joe Pig'sEar at Newcastle and now Paul Hart in charge at Pompey. According to my brother Gus Hiddink was chosen for the Chelsea job from a shortlist that also included David Platt, Harry Bassett and Frank Clark. I think he might be winding me up.

February 22nd

(The following entry was written after our 3-1 away league victory against Forest)
I didn't go to Saturday's match unfortunately so had to make do with the radio.

Whilst listening to us humiliate Forest in their own backyard, there were two particularly poor pieces of commentary. The first was by Ross Fletcher on

Radio Derby: about half an hour in with the Rams leading 1-0 he asked Gary Rowett "so Gary, which of the two managers will be happier at this stage?" I'll give you a clue Ross, it wasn't Billy Davies.

My son woke up towards the end of the match so I had to go upstairs and discovered that I could only get Ram FM (for readers out the area, this is a station the Mark and Lard phrase "tin pot local radio" could have been invented for). After Nyatanga was taken off, the commentator started discussing the number of defenders injured, beginning with Alan Stubbs. I hope he's not expecting him back? I can just imagine in three years time "we're here at the Bernabeu for Real Madrid v. The Rams, Alan Stubbs is *still* injured".

February 23rd

I noticed from Saturday that Forest assistant manager David Kelly has joined the select bunch who likes to be known by his nickname, with "NED" on his training kit. (Other members being P'Ince asking to be known as "the Guv'nor" and Neil Ruddock telling Liverpool team-mates to call him "Razor". Legend has it the Liverpool players stuck strictly to "Neil" afterwards).

According to someone who commented on the Times column, NED is actually an acronym for Never Ever Delivered.

February 25th

I was challenged by the Hull Fan At Work recently about a mention of drinking Pear Cider in Bad Worse Worst (what he actually said was "every time I watch The Championship and the adverts come on, I think 'who drinks this stuff?' Now I know" - the programme is sponsored by St. Helliers Pear Cider). He was quick to point out that Pear Cider a.k.a. Perry is basically Babycham repackaged and remarketed. A female colleague said how nice Pear Cider is, to back me up. It was well intended but didn't really strengthen my argument.

The next time I was in Sainsbury's, I looked at the cider: the first rack contained the standard Strongbow, Dry Blackthorn etc., with Quite Frightening and the likes at the bottom. The second rack had all the gourmet ciders, moving on to Pear Cider, then Perry and sure enough, tucked away at the bottom was Babycham!

I've now got a bottle, courtesy of my next door neighbours, and was saving it for a special occasion. I think the car journey to Doncaster on Friday could be ideal.

February 28th

♫ There's only one Gary Teale, one Gary Teale, he used to be shite but now he's alright, walking in a Teale wonderland ♫
A bit harsh on Teale in my opinion but quite funny nonetheless.
When you contrast the two Doncaster defeats, it's amazing what a bit of feel-good factor can bring. Obviously the first game of the season was at home with a huge weight of expectation but even so, a lot of people would have been happy to see Jagger tarred and feathered (along with half the team) after the August defeat. On Friday, defeat was met with some disappointment but a general feeling of "you can't win 'em all". Savage's goal was the only highlight. As the free kick was being lined up, I fancied him to score. With almost scripted timing I asked my brother "Savage has never scored for us has he?" to which he replied "...he has now". Boom! Boom!

I can confirm that Babycham is basically a slightly acidic Pear Cider (see Journals 25th February). Maybe it would have tasted a better with a glacé cherry rammed in the top?

The Rams were blighted by injury problems for the final leg of the season

"You play the first half and I'll play the second"

PART 4

"We are limping along to the end of the season."

Nigel Clough April 2009

The final phase of the season was characterised by several injuries to key players, news of which was often followed by "…and is out for the rest of the season". Miles Addison had limped off against Blackpool in February and was not to be seen again; Paul Green and Chris Porter's season ended in early March; McEveley's shoulder ruled him out for large spells; Leacock was already out for the season; and Steve Davies' season also ended prematurely. With niggling injuries and suspensions contributing, The Rams had little continuity compared to the previous run that had been built around stability.

Addison and Green were both contenders for Player of the Year so were sorely missed. Chris Porter was also missed after he had lived up to Clough's billing with three goals in as many starts. Porter looked an uncomplicated player who knew where the net was - a stark contrast to others who had tried and failed. In just three games, Porter had already matched Ellington's league total and surpassed Villa and Varney.

Clough was able to bring two loan players in: John Eustace from Watford and youngster Barry Bannan from Aston Villa. By Clough's own admission, a key factor in signing Eustace was that he was simply available.

The exit door was also swinging again with two of Jewell's forward signings heading out the door. Luke Varney surprisingly joined Sheffield Wednesday and Liam Dickinson joined Leeds United in his third loan spell of the season.

After a spell of adventurous attacking football, The Rams were forced to become more pragmatic and results driven. The Rams were not entirely clear of the relegation pack so needed to keep the points tally ticking over. The scrappy home victory against Bristol City, in which City had eighteen shots to Derby's eight, was typical of the resilience Clough had tried to instil.

Unfortunately, old problems were beginning to resurface and The Rams lost heavily away to play-off contenders Sheffield United and Cardiff (4-2 and 4-1 respectively). Derby's scrappy late own goal at Cardiff ultimately cost Cardiff a play-off place as they missed out by a single goal.

Burton Albion's promotion challenge…

As the Rams season began to peter out, much local attention turned to the fortunes of Clough's ex-team Burton Albion. Clough has presided over a steady climb through the football pyramid for Burton, having taken the Brewers from the old Southern Premier League to the top of the Conference National. Clough left Burton eleven victories into to a Conference record run of twelve straight wins.

Burton had been as much as 19 points clear at one stage, so in theory all manager Roy McFarland had to do was see the Brewers over the finishing line and into the Football League for the first time in the clubs history. However, things did not go to plan. With the finishing line in sight, Burton began to stumble with a pack of teams behind them eagerly biting at the Brewers heels. Burton managed only four victories in the remaining fourteen matches. The elusive "couple more wins" never came and the Brewers lost five of their final six fixtures, including the final three, when one point would have been sufficient.

Fortunately for Burton, closest rivals Cambridge United surprisingly drew 0-0 at home on the final day when a victory would have decided the title on goal difference.

...and back to The Rams

As the season headed towards its conclusion, one win in March had meant The Rams were still not mathematically safe from relegation. A scrappy win at Sheffield Wednesday provided some breathing space but this was followed by three consecutive defeats. Old problems of weak defending were back to haunt The Rams as goal after goal was conceded with minimum resistance. More injuries gave greater opportunity to fringe players allowing Clough and fans alike to see that players such as Sterjovski, Todd, Villa and Kazmierczak were not players to take the Rams forward. Ellington and Stewart had disappeared from the picture entirely whilst early season star Martin Albrechtsen suffered a massive dip in form.

The Rams won twice in April, the aforementioned Sheffield Wednesday game and against relegated Charlton in the final home fixture. Both games finished 1-0 with Rob Hulse scoring the single goal on each occasion. Hulse collected the Player of the Year award before the Charlton match and those two games alone exemplified the importance of Hulse's contribution over the season. Clough asked one final favour of Rob Hulse for the final match of the season and Hulse finished the campaign as a makeshift central defender in the 1-3 defeat at Watford.

The Damned United

March 2009 saw the release of the film version of David Peace's The Damned United, the story of Brian Clough's 44 days in charge of Leeds United. The book had created a lot of controversy locally for its portrayal of Brian Clough and the Clough family spoke out publicly against the portrayal of Clough as a heavy-drinking, dark, complex character.

The films release was accompanied by a blaze of publicity both locally and nationally. Other Clough related projects also appeared (a play, a TV documentary and other publications) often with the tag-line of telling the *real* Clough story. The Damned United has been heavily criticised by both fans and ex-players of Derby and Leeds United but there is no doubt that it was a catalyst for the huge amount of, mostly positive, Clough tributes witnessed during 2009.

The film itself was a stark contrast to the book. Whilst the book was dark, broody, introspective and at times challenging; the film was very light-hearted with an almost camp portrayal of characters and events. The Derby County of the 1970's featured heavily in the film with a consistently positive depiction of Clough and the club. It seems a pity that possibly the only mainstream production to feature the Rams so heavily would be missed by the very people who would beam with pride on viewing it.

The Damned United

Despite its critical acclaim, The Damned United was not well received by all Rams fans

Journals of Derventio – March to May 2009

March 2nd

The trailers for The Damned United have been doing the rounds for a couple of weeks now.

Apparently Saltergate has been mocked up as the Baseball Ground; from the brief snippets on the clip, it looks like a decent job has been done. I'm no film expert so I was surprised to hear that Clough is played by the same actor (Michael Sheen) chosen to portray Kenneth Williams!
(Thanks to Lee for much of the above)

March 4th

A joke from the Hull Fan At Work today:
Q. What's the difference between Phil Brown and God?
A. God doesn't think he's Phil Brown.
Ouch! It seems the tide of the North Sea has turned a bit for Brownie. It was only a few months ago when the Hull Fan At Work was showing me a Tigers website featuring pictures of Brown's brown shoes! Now that is hero worship (or were they just ridiculing his shoes? who knows).

After Hull's recent dip, it seems that Craig Fagan is now their top striker. I suggested a Fagan version of the Teale chant may be appropriate...

March 5th

A reader emailed me a link to a story about Peschisolido becoming Galway's assistant manager; the Irish clubs current manager being Jeff Kenna. I'd heard this mentioned before and my first thought was: why would a player with a relatively successful career (i.e. quite a few signing-on fees), who is married to one of the countries most famous businesswomen, with several kids, move abroad to become no.2 in one of Europe's weakest leagues? I don't know the answer, just thought I'd pose the question. (If you do know, try this one: why would Craig Short blah, blah, million pound transfers, blah, blah, sailing business, blah, blah Hungarian second division. See Journals January 5th if you don't get this).

You may recall that Pesch and Jeff were briefly part of Terry Westley's crisis management team after the Phil Brown debacle, which also coincided with the end of Jeff's playing days. It always amuses me to think of the three of them discussing improving the side:
Westley: I've been racking my brains lads, I can't think of any decent full-backs at the club.
Pesch: Neither can I Tez, they're all shite. Let's bring in Alan Wright on loan.
Jeff: I'll get me trackie top.

As the reader, Dr. Andy, pointed out, Pesch's comment of: 'We talked a lot at Derby about the way we would do things if we ever had the chance of working at a club together.' Basically translates as "when we used to slag Phil Brown off"
(The Pesch comment was featured on an Irish football site).

March 8th

(The following entry refers to The Rams v. Bristol City match at Pride Park. The match was switched to a lunch-time kick-off on Police advice because Forest were hosting Swansea on the same day).
Football is rarely seen as a champion of minority interests but for once, the football league decided to favour the small man. As a result, 31,000 people were inconvenienced for the benefit of a smaller gathering 16 miles away. I don't know if trouble was anticipated at Pride Park but as I walked past the back of the away

end, there were banks of heavily armed Police with nothing to do. To pass the time, one young teenage Bristol City fan, in replica shirt and jeans, was being given a body search as thorough as possible with bare hands. Given the level of security, I was fully expecting the Sri Lankan cricket team to be doing the half-time Goldrush draw.

(The Sri Lankan cricket team had just withdrawn from a Test series in Pakistan after their team coach had been attacked).

A text I sent to Bob around kick-off ended "...let's see what Bruce Sterjovski can do". Seconds later, he'd skinned four players and we'd scored. I pledged to try the trick again and after half an hour sent: "let's see what J-Mac can do". Seconds later J-Mac sliced a left-wing cross out for a goal kick.

Even in the space of a few weeks, Nigel Clough has shown an impressive knack of diagnosing a problem and solving it (e.g. we need to get more crosses in). When we signed Chris Porter, Clough said that we needed someone who was currently scoring goals despite already having a glut of strikers: the skilful maverick Nathan Ellington (3 league goals in 13 starts and 13 sub appearances); million pound speedster Luke Varney (1 goal, 6 starts, 1 sub); and the fans favourite, £2m Tito Villa (2 goals, 12 starts, 12 sub). No frills Chris Porter arrives - 3 goals in 3 starts. Hats off to Clough.

Bristol City will no doubt be gutted after Saturday but in a fair and just world, we'd have got a point at Doncaster, beaten Swansea and lost to Bristol - four points. It's no consolation to Bristol City but it's some proof of the theory that luck evens itself out. We still ended up with four points from the three games.

March 9th

The Damned United debate seems to be building up a head of steam in preparation for the films release. I particularly liked an article in the Telegraph about John McGovern titled "They're cashing in on Clough". It begins with

McGovern saying that The Damned United shouldn't have been published and that David Peace was just cashing in on Clough's name. McGovern then goes onto say how he was at the film set cracking jokes and advising players - possibly the worst boycott ever.

Next paragraph: "McGovern was speaking at the launch of Brian Clough's Way, a stage celebration of his life.." more cashing in on Clough's name or a genre defying work of art? I don't know I haven't seen it. McGovern's final comment in the "Cashing in on Clough" article was "...I'll be happy to be there wherever and whenever I'm wanted". For free I assume, wouldn't want to cash in John.

Discussing the McGovern article, I came across a couple of amusing anecdotes. Before I carry on, I don't know McGovern as man or player and I've no reason to believe he's anything less than a fine example of both. Anyway, first one...

A few years ago, McGovern was assistant manager of Hull but after keeping them in the football league on a shoestring, was unjustly sacked. Shortly after, he was manager of Ilkeston Town. In the bar after a match, he was signing bits and pieces of Derby and Forest memorabilia before the Hull Fan At Work thrust a Hull programme in front of him. Apparently, John's faced dropped like stone. The Hull Fan had to convince him that it wasn't a wind up before the programme was begrudgingly signed.

The second story: at a fans forum, again in Ilkeston, McGovern, Archie Gemmill and Rory Delap were fielding questions from supporters. Simon had given Archie the Spanish Inquisition by asking: "Is it true that we signed the wrong player when Carbonari joined?" (rumours were circulating at the time that the player that arrived was not the one scouted) and "Why did we sign Mikel Beck when Jim Smith went on record as saying Beck was not a player that interested us, when offered in a deal for Sturridge?".

When asked: "who was the best player you've ever played with?" Rory Delap began singing the praises of Matt Jansen. The host said "that ties in nicely with this gentleman's question" (Simon was limbering up to ask "Why didn't we sign Matt Jansen when we had him on trial?"), McGovern could be heard muttering "bloody hell, it's Magnus Magnusson again". After a dose of loudmouth soup, Simon said his farewell to McGovern in the car park with a shout of "has Shilts paid you back yet!" (a reference to rumours at the time that McGovern had helped Peter Shilton sort out some debts. McGovern had recently been Shilts' assistant at Plymouth).

March 11th

A selection of comments from Forest fans after the Watford defeat, taken from the Notts Post website:
"I have never been a fan of Billy D and I think we are better without him than with him."
"Message to Billy and Lorraine Kelly:
Pick up your ego's the giant bag of excuses and your platform shoes and GO..... just go !"
"That's it Billy, blame the players. Never mind that you shuffled them around like a deck of cards. Admit you got it wrong and maybe you get some respect."
That's three of the first four. There are roughly sixty others beneath that.

March 12th

I'm all for innocent until proven guilty and all that; but when you read "Mackay, 53 of Alicante", you have to wonder don't you?
(a reference to the trial of ex-Rams Directors Jeremy Keith, Murdo Mackay and Andrew Mackenzie for various financial irregularities. All three were found guilty)

March 15th

I wrote last month (Feb 19th) about the strange phenomenon of axed Forest managers landing Premier League jobs after Joe Kinnear and Paul Hart were appointed to save Newcastle and Portsmouth respectively. (I forgot the groundbreaking Gary Megson). Well, it seems the trend continues with Colin Calderwood being taken on by Newcastle to assist in the absence of the aforementioned Kinnear. Or as the Daily Mirror puts it:
"Mike Ashley is taking a £50million gamble by entrusting Newcastle's fight for survival to Colin Calderwood and Chris Hughton.". It seems Calderwood will be the senior partner according to the Mirror: "Former Nottingham Forest boss Calderwood is expected to take interim charge, assisted by Hughton...Hughton was a disaster as caretaker boss – Newcastle lost all four games when he stepped into the void left by Kevin Keegan's departure in September."

After Forest's most recent debacle at Burnley *(a 5-0 defeat)*, Billy Davies is thought to be watching Rafa Benitez's protracted contract talks with interest.

March 16th

No sooner had we signed Barry Bannan on loan from Villa than the Journals inbox was prodded into action...one of our regular correspondence has encountered Barry on-line. Now, before you get onto the News of the World, there's no need to worry - it was during an online game of Football Manager and I'm assured that Baz is quite adept at "computer management sims". More importantly, Bannan is apparently genuinely excited to be joining us and getting some first team football. I don't think "genuinely excited" were words ever uttered by Emerson Thome or Stern John on arrival.

March 18th

You may be wondering about the welfare of Giles Barnes with him not playing for Fulham. Well, wonder no more, our Journals spies report that he is alive and well, or to be more accurate "with two blonde girls…one on each arm. He looked happy enough". So where was the Premier League star sighted? Chinawhites? Legends? the Nuts Awards? No. In student digs in Leeds.

Amateur psychologists and cynics among you may be drawing parallels with Giles' football career here i.e. it's easier to shine when the opposition is a bit weaker. (No offence intended students, I've been there myself and the sad reality is that someone dripping in bling with several grand of loose change is more likely to end up "with two blondes…one on each arm" than your average student in a band t-shirt and £10 budget for the night). The added bonus for Barnes is that Jermaine Defoe is unlikely to turn up in Leeds Student Union packing a bigger wedge and a few England anecdotes.

March 21st

Around this time last year, the Rams launched an advertising campaign for season tickets featuring several members of the first team squad, supplemented by a couple of black lads from the youth team. I commented at the time that this did not bode well for the futures of Jonno, Big Dave, Fagan, Davis, Mears and Earnie. Even if I say so myself - it wasn't a bad call.

Approaching the stadium today, I saw a new advertising campaign entitled "Strike Force", featuring Commons, Hulse, Porter and Davies. The Duke, Tito Dicko and Varney are gathering their belongings as we speak.

On a related topic - I went to my dad's for tea on Friday and we were talking about Varney. I was saying "he couldn't get a game at bottom-of-the-league Charlton, we pay a million quid for him and they replace him with Sheffield Wednesday (and Rams) reject Deon Burton." Half an hour later we both got a text from my brother saying that Varney had joined Sheffield Wednesday on loan - presumably to replace Deon Burton.

One of the clubs in this equation has ended up with neither money nor player.

March 23rd

The Damned United publicity has given rise to no end of Clough snr. articles. The BBC even ran one recently titled "What if Brian Clough were your office manager?", the premise being to translate Clough's management into today's office environment. Far from being a light hearted, tongue-in-cheek piece; the BBC enlisted "Professor Stefan Szymanski, of the Cass Business School, and Murray Steele, senior lecturer at the Cranfield School of Management, [to] examine how Clough's skills might have transferred into business."

The article clutches at several straws in an attempt to make the concept work, with a particularly bad bit under the heading of "Always look out for talent": The following is a direct copy and paste of consecutive paragraphs with no manipulation by me for comic effect:
"And if Clough spotted something in Claire, currently languishing in IT, he would go to extraordinary lengths to ensure her departmental transfer.
Prof Symanski explains how Clough would go to the house of his target to talk to them about a proposed move. If they weren't there, he would stay the night, even offering to help do the washing up and the cooking while he waited."

Imagine: you spot "Claire in IT", go to her house, stay the night, start washing up and cooking etc.

The chances are next morning you will be greeted by your companies HR and the Police. One was brandishing a P45, the other a restraining order.

March 24th

Adrian Chiles - football enthusiast. Is he the real deal? If so, why does he go to games with Frank Skinner instead of his "real footie mates from back in the day"? The reason I ask is that he apparently committed a real football faux pas yesterday - he referred to us as "Derby City".

To be fair to him, I got his book (titled "We Don't Know What We're Doing") for Christmas and he does seem genuine and passionate about West Brom. However, that's not to say his passion makes interesting reading - it's one of the few books I've given up on.

It's basically the story of West Brom's relegation season in 2005/6. He starts by enthusiastically boarding the coach to away matches but by September he's opting to watch matches live in the comfort of the Match of The Day studios, thus completely undermining his I'm-just-like-you persona (especially when he's accompanied by the aforementioned Frank Skinner). It also gets a bit far fetched at times - The Duke scores a brace in the Premier League.

March 26th

I notice in the Barometer *(a Ramspace feature)* that there is a reference to Stephen Bywater cage-fighting. In the March issue of FourFourTwo it actually quotes Bywater as saying that he'd like to go into cage-fighting when he retires from football and has sounded his agent out about it.

Ironic really, as I'd previously written how level-headed he seems to be nowadays. Goalkeepers are usually in their upper thirties when they retire, most opt for the occasional round of golf, spending time with their kids or maybe a coaching badge. Bywater wants to spend his forties, semi-naked fighting grown men in a confined space. Fair enough and best of luck to him. More exciting than being a smug overweight TV pundit I suppose (although I wouldn't mind seeing a Bywater TV career. A stint on Big Brother maybe? More likely the inaugural "Celebrity Cage-Fighting" on ITV20).

March 30th

Simon has pointed out that last weekend was one of the less celebrated Rams anniversaries - it was this time last year that the Rams were relegated after our home draw against Fulham. I remember leaving the ground and being unaware that we had finally gone. Ever the optimist, my mind was more occupied with the thought of Tito Villa tearing-up the Championship after his Premier League brace.

As if you need reminding how bad we were, Simon made the point that Luton are still making a fist of it in League Two despite starting the season with a whopping 30 point deduction and a threadbare squad. They are currently on 22 points, double our final tally last year, with seven games to go.

(Luton were eventually relegated but not before winning the Football League trophy at Wembley)

April 2nd

Could The Rams be getting a new celebrity fan? In an interview in the Observer Sport magazine, Michael Sheen (Clough in the Damned United) said:
"...I'm now thinking of becoming a fully fledged Derby fan [...] I find myself listening out for Derby's results and going to the back pages of the paper and looking to see how they played. And I was jokingly thinking that I would donate money from the film to buy a new back four, because I know Nigel is very unhappy with his defenders".

I haven't seen the film yet but it looks like its quite clear who the good guys are. There'd be something wrong if he was saying "I'm thinking of becoming a Leeds fan"!

April 5th

(Written after the 1-1 home draw with Burnley. Paul Connolly scored an injury time equaliser for The Rams).
I managed to tempt fate with a text for the second time yesterday (the first being before the Bristol City game- Journals March 8th). Connolly has been a bit dodgy recently and yesterday was no exception; without being shocking he was showing all the hallmarks of being a lower division full-back, rather than one who will take us (or even captain us) to the next level. His nadir came during the latter stages when a long Burnley punt was sailing out for a Derby throw-in. Connolly, for reasons unknown, tried to control the ball but made such a hash of it that it didn't even bounce off him. He missed it completely prompting me to send a text that I never thought I would: "Bring Mears back!".
Five minutes later: "Connolly...GOAL!"

April 6th

After a couple of quiet weeks, Billy Davies is up to his old antics again. This time being accused of playing mind-games with Barnsley before last Saturday's fixture. Barnsley manager Simon Davey said Davies was bordering on bringing the game into disrepute by saying that Sheffield Utd's Chris Morgan "embodied the attitude and approach he wanted to see in his side" (quotation from the Observer not Billy Davies). Earlier this season Chris Morgan fractured the skull of Barnsley's £1.2m striker Iain Hume.

Davies defended himself by saying that, when asked about the type of player he'd like to bring to the club, he said "Chris Lucketti and Chris Morgan -

their type of mentality and experience". But how genuine was Davies' response? Only last week I read on the BBC "Huddersfield Town...have told Chris Lucketti to look for another club". A player being turfed out by a League One surely couldn't have been too costly? Or maybe he didn't get the green light from Forest's infamous "acquisition committee"? Who knows. If Davies was just referring to his halcyon days at Preston, he should have just taken Clod when he was up for grabs.

April 8th

I went to see The Damned United on Tuesday. I won't attempt a full film review but I thought there were a few points of particular interest to Rams fans:

1) I've heard a few people say that they aren't going to watch the film because the Clough family and some ex-players were quite offended by the book. A fair enough principle to hold but, for better or worse, the film is nothing like the book. Whereas the book is dark, intense and portrays Clough as a very complex man; the film is generally very light, very pro-Derby and pro-Clough. Don't *not* go on principle, you'd be denying yourself a good night.

2) The book has never claimed to be the complete truth but does stick to the objective facts e.g. scores, dates etc. The film however, strays from the facts a few times. Most notably showing Derby playing Leeds a few days before facing Juventus in the European Cup semi-final. The Rams get kicked off the park and the defeat to Juventus is attributed to having to play a near reserve team - the whole affair is the source of a major falling out between Clough and Sam Longston. In reality, the Derby v. Leeds match was a month before the Juventus game, where the Rams fielded a full strength team. With so much genuine material, it seems a pity to create pure fiction. (Facts confirmed by my brother thanks to Derby County - The Complete Record).

3) Derby are consistently portrayed as the good guys and any Rams fan would feel proud to see it. It's a shame that there was so much negativity being peddled before the films release. Now if you were a Leeds fan you might have just cause for complaint. The film-makers goodwill towards Derby even extends to the final credits - during a "what happened next" sequence, Forest are introduced as a "small provincial club"!

April 12th

(Written after Derby's 1-0 victory at Hillsborough)
Sheffield Wednesday yesterday was a rare outing for a few of us, to celebrate my brother's birthday earlier in the week. It nearly got off to the worst possible start; we arrived in Sheffield to be met by a group of police. One of them asked Simon "are you Derby County fans?" to which he immediately replied with no hint of sarcasm "no, we're just doing some shopping". To my astonishment, the seven of us were allowed to pass. To be fair, it could have just been some common sense by the PC in question, reasoning that a group including my 61 year old dad weren't about to start a Wild West brawl. I'm not sure what the consequences were for being a Rams fan in Sheffield at that time but I assume they weren't handing out free tickets.

Once past the barricades, we were able to enjoy a civilised time around Sheffield but for the first few hundred yards, there were literally police on every corner. The Damned United was discussed at length with Simon's analysis being: "Brokeback Mountain set in the East Midlands". As soon as he said it, I thought of the scene where Peter Taylor was feeding crisps into the mouth of a laughing Brian Clough; homoerotica if ever I saw it.

The match itself was instantly forgettable. I do occasionally forget major incidents after a couple of pre-match drinks but I'm quite sure that nothing at all happened apart from Hulse's goal. To use a musical analogy: The Horrors have recently described their new album as "...like going to the top of a really tall hill with your best friends on the most beautiful summer's day and taking a load of really good E and then running down the hill really fast". Well, yesterday's win was like drinking a can of Trent Bitter then running down Ilkeston's disused ski-slope on a murky day. It was fine within the parameters you're working with.

I'm not complaining though; an away win at Hillsborough and a tidy coupon win all adds up to a good day out (the bookies were offering a generous 13/5 on a Rams victory). The day was paid for and there was still enough left in the kitty for a team bottle of M&S pink shampoo for the train journey home.

April 14th

Companies often employ third-party call centres to deal with a particular piece of work or when some extra capacity is needed. The trick is for the call centre to be absolutely convincing that they are the company they are merely representing. The company employed to deal with telephone season ticket renewals failed to do this at least twice.

First up: Bob rang to renew and was told there would be a £10 charge (presumably to pay for the aforementioned call centre). After a lengthy debate about the validity of the phone-tax, the facade suddenly dropped: "you'll have to complain to Derby County" prompting the obvious question: "well who are you then?"

Second example: Simon rang up to renew and was similarly surprised to be hit by the stealth tax. His response was "ok, hold it there, I'll be down in half an hour" (conscious that the cost of the call was ticking over like a taxi-meter). He then asked "is it busy?" to which the answer came "erm...erm..I don't know", so he suggested "well, look out the window, are there many people around?" to be told "erm, I'm not actually there".

It could have been worse I told him, pressing the wrong option could have landed you with a subscription to Chelsea TV or a new broadband package.

April 15th

It seems I have written something of interest; imagine my surprise at work today when browsing the Telegraph website, there was yesterdays Journals in the "latest posts on the forums" section. Someone had started a thread by copying and pasting the whole entry. I don't mind at all and I'm really pleased that someone found it of interest; I just wanted to make the point that it wasn't me doing some guerrilla marketing for the site! There are a couple of comments on the thread, one which reveals that the third party company are seetickets. It's annoying enough when they charge a couple of quid admin fee when you're buying a gig ticket, never mind a Jeff* when you're trying to buy a season ticket!
*Kenna - tenner

April 16th

Further to yesterdays entry about seetickets handling Rams telephone season ticket sales (and charging a tenner), a reader contacted us to say that his mate had got, shall we say, "a real bargain". Presumably the super-efficient teleseller was pre-occupied simultaneously selling Dancing on Ice tickets on another line. Well, we'll see if he's still so pleased with himself when he has to turn up in August with a stick-on grey beard and flat cap. It could be that Tom Glick included a few Willy Wonka tickets but I'm sure he'd have mentioned it.

(Now there's a marketing idea: "Renew your season ticket before May 31 and you may receive a Golden Ticket. This could be exchanged for a) a drive around Donnington in Robbie Savage's car b) a cage fight with Stephen Bywater or c) a night out with Liam Dickinson. Please note - Derby County's insurance will not cover you for any of the aforementioned activities")

April 19th

One of the nominees for this years Sunday Times Young Writer of the Year was Derby born Edward Hogan for his novel Blackmoor. Unfortunately he didn't win, which is a shame as not only is it a great read but one of the few books ever to be set in and around Derbyshire.

One of the pivotal parts of the book is when a fire starts in an old pit village and starts burning an unmined coal seam. It's here that Hogan shows his roots - the fire is started by someone setting fire to a Forest shirt!

April 20th

AZ Alkmaar have won the Dutch title for only the second time in their history after a 28 year gap. They are managed by ex-Barcelona boss Louis van Gaal who finished 11th with them last season and lost the first two games of this campaign. I'll let BBC Sport take up the story:

"Things swiftly changed and Van Gaal's master stroke was uncovering a key player in prolific Moroccan striker Mounir El Hamdaoui, who scored his 22nd league goal on Saturday in AZ's 2-1 home defeat by Vitesse Arnhem."

So El Hamdaoui is Champions League bound; or more likely, he'll sign for a mid-table Premier League side for in excess of £10m.

(From the Journals November 6th 2007: "Mounir El Hamdaoui has now signed for UEFA Cup qualifiers AZ Alkmaar. A decent step up for saying he had yet another injury ravaged season last year, playing just 7 games for Willem II.")

April 22nd

El Hamdaoui update - according to my brother, the latest edition of World Soccer reports that Barcelona are tracking him!

I mentioned the story to the Hull Fan At Work the other day and his response was: "you're telling me Phil Brown knew about this bloke all along". Incidentally, I was reading a Hull fanzine and one of the contributors named his favoured line-up - Craig Fagan was the lone striker. Hard times at the KC Stadium.

April 23rd

(Written before the Charlton home match, when defensive injuries were really taking their toll). My brother and I were discussing the possible defensive permutations for Saturday if Todd is declared unfit. It was a short conversation. Last nights reserve match might provide some clues: Jason Beardsley played left-back (no great shock) and... wait for it... Tito Villa played centre-back! Now let's briefly consider Tito's qualities: decent in the air; tackles like nutter; doesn't mind splitting his head open in the challenge; no great skill or craft on the ball. Exactly what our defence has been crying out for weeks! Maybe Tito does have a future after all?

Onto other topics, Tyrone Mears is touting himself for a move to England. The story is on the Telegraph website but the gist is that Mears wants a move to England for family reasons, ideally to a club matching Marseille's achievements (i.e. title contenders, Champions League next season etc.) to which Adam Pearson quite rightly says he needs to be more realistic.

A few weeks ago there was a lot of press about Mears scoring in the UEFA Cup and breaking into the Marseille team at last. According to his agent, half of Europe were trying to sign him. According to the latest story, he has lost his place already after just four games, to a youngster. It's worth adding to the story that Marseille aren't seeing out the season and giving a kid a run out; they are currently four points clear at the top of Ligue1 and chasing down their first title for 17 years*. In other words, playing their strongest team possible. Are Marseille going to spend a million quid on a third choice right-back? I think Forest is a more likely destination.

*Marseille were pipped by Bordeaux whilst Tyrone Mears joined Premier League newcomers Burnley.

April 25th

The season at Pride Park closed in a similar fashion to how it began - a disappointing match decided by a single goal. The good news was that The Rams got the goal and I had a "home win" on my winning coupon.

As the match petered out, events off the pitch became more interesting as the stewards and police tried to cope with the inevitable pitch invasion. With about five minutes remaining, a group of mainly teenage lads started a conga along the front of the East Stand. Meanwhile at the away end, approximately 30 stewards were crouched in front of Charlton's following of about 300 (none of which had shown any inclination to "get down the front").

Just before the final whistle, the bloke on the tannoy asked fans not to come on the pitch. A few Charlton fans wandered to the front ready to greet their players and suddenly, the stewards were supplemented by almost as many police - it looked like a G20 protest without the protesters.

When the whistle blew, fans predictably swarmed on the pitch. The stadium announcer was now in a muddle - follow the party line or play the crowd pleaser? In a schizophrenic display, he played Black Lace's "Come on and do the conga", interrupted it to ask fans to leave the pitch and then carried on with the conga! Needless to say, no one left the pitch. For me, it's all part and parcel of the last game: walk on the pitch, say "how can anyone mis-control a ball / slice a corner / not play a ten yard pass etc. on this surface?"; bump into a few random acquaintances; then go home.

Leaving the stadium, we saw a few players and Simon decided to add Tito Villa to his stalkers gallery. Unfortunately, Simon's camera was playing up, leaving him standing with his arm round Tito for an uncomfortably long time whilst I tried in vain to take the photo. After fixing the problem, we then dragged Tito away from a conversation to try again. I have to say, he was the perfect gent for his patience during all this buffoonery.

April 28th

Phil Brown has finally broke his silence on a rumour that's been circulating since his Derby days if not before. In Saturdays Guardian he insisted "...I've never been on a sunbed in my entire life. It's just that I take the rays very easily".

The article, advertised as "The madness of Phil Brown" on the front of the sport supplement, discusses Hull's rise and fall during the season. It grandly attributes Hull's early season success to "a confusingly kaleidoscopic array of formations...an audaciously attacking Hull mixed cleverly choreographed set pieces with some surprisingly sweet passing".

The Hull Fan at Work assures me that "confusingly kaleidoscopic formations" can still be seen at the KC. This roughly translates as "no one knows what they're doing or where they're playing".

May 3rd

The season's over thank goodness - let the squad cull commence. Here are a few points of interest from the Observer's fans review of 2008/9:

Only one Derby player featured in any clubs "Top five opposition players" - Blackpool included Chris Commons. Not surprising really given his goals against them this season. Marcus Tudgay features in two teams "Top 5's" and was also given a rapturous write-up by the Sheff Wednesday fan.

Derby fans were declared to be the best away fans by both Sheffield clubs, with the Wednesday fan generously writing "...very warm, welcoming and loud - the craic was excellent". I can't imagine that I would be so kind after a dire home defeat, so credit to him.

Robbie Savage was chosen as "Top hate figure at another club" by two teams: Forest (predictably) and Plymouth. He must be mellowing.

For the same category, the Derby writer chose a manager from another midlands club...Mick McCarthy. "It dates back to his days as Millwall manager. I find him smug" was the explanation. Well, he wasn't very smug when we beat them in the Play-off semi's was he?

May 6th

I've heard it said a few times (but never officially) that a condition of our adidas kit deal is that we have a clean sweep every year and introduce three new kits, required or not* (does the "Argentina" kit avoid any clashes incurred by the white home shirt that our away kit wouldn't? does anyone play in white and slime green stripes?). With 50% off kits at the moment, it looks likely that we'll be getting the 7th, 8th and 9th kit within the space of three years. Tom Glick is currently looking at a Dulux test card for new colours.

With the pressure on to shift the stock, I had the following text forwarded on from Bob: "DCFC sent me a voucher for a free 08/09 away shirt...'cause it's bright slime green it makes an excellent hi-viz when I ride my push bike to work. I'm quite chuffed..."

I'm convinced half of our goals conceded away from home last season were due to stewards and police playing the striker on-side.

*It was confirmed in June 2009 that the adidas deal requires two new kits per season, not three.

The season that was

In spite of The Rams humiliating relegation in 2008, the season started with some optimism. A squads worth of new players had arrived and Paul Jewell was bullish about our chances of promotion. By 16.50pm on August 9th 2008, much of the initial optimism had drained from over 30,000 Rams fans who had just witnessed a home defeat to Doncaster.

Results did gradually pick up but it became clear that Jewell's newly assembled side were not likely to be challenging for promotion. A brief flirtation with lower play-off places in autumn was as good as it got. Jewell's post-match interviews frequently revealed his frustration that he could not quite get the mix right as new signings such as Kazmierczak, Dickinson, Varney and Ellington, were not contributing as anticipated; and previously signings Savage, Stubbs, Villa and Sterjovski were hardly contributing at all.

Jewell's parting statement as quoted by the club: "[he] feels he is no longer in a position to take the club forward" summed up the situation perfectly. It was clear The Rams would need overhauling once more.

A welcome distraction from the indifferent league form was the Carling Cup run. The headline victory – the home win over Manchester United – came after Jewell's departure, meaning that Jewell was denied his moment in the sun after a horrible year in charge. It was a shame that Jewell missed this final crumb of comfort; despite a disastrous year, Jewell was generally well-liked amongst Rams fans and it was widely acknowledged he had a near impossible job on his hands from the outset. The Carling Cup run had seen Jewell negotiate some tricky matches along the way and The Rams appalling cup form in the past 30 years (last major semi-final 1976) highlighted Jewell's achievements.

The phrase "a new era" is massively overused both in football and in life. However, it is no exaggeration to say that the appointment of Nigel Clough is the beginning of a new era for The Rams. Fans recognise that after a procession of managers in the past decade, stability and long term building is needed. Nigel Clough proved at Burton that, given the right backing, he is capable of building gradually, avoiding the boom and bust that has ruined many a football club in recent years and also left the Rams heavily indebted in the past.

An important ingredient in the plan is the fans. Many managers have joined new clubs with the announcement "I've got a three year plan" but how many have the chance to see it through? Supporters and chairman rarely have the patience. However, with Clough, it feels as though Rams fans do have some faith and will have the patience to see what happens. Maybe it's the "Clough" name, or maybe we have had enough of the short-termism that has seen a rash of high-cost-low-quality signings over the past few years. Clough has already proved his preference for longevity with a ten-year stint at Burton Albion.

With a stable manager, apparent financial stability and seemingly growing fanbase, could the good ship of Derby County finally be leaving choppy waters?

"There was a kind of sinking feeling when you first walked in here. I think we have stopped that and can look forward to next season."

Rob Hulse May 2009

Extra Time...

The article below is based on a piece I wrote for the Ramspace website after the Rams decided to restructure the youth academy. The article refers to young debutants Mark Dudley and Mark O'Brien who both came on as substitutes in the last game off the season at Watford.

Lame Academy

As the season closes, 2008/9 becomes the third consecutive season that the Rams have not had a home-grown debutant starting a league game – that's no one since Barnes, Nyatanga and Addison were introduced in the Brown/ Westley era in 2005/6.

The end of the season also coincides with the departure of academy boss Phil Cannon, making room for the fourth different academy regime in as many years. Blame the managers; blame the academy bosses; blame the scouts; blame the players for being simply not good enough – draw your own conclusions but these are the facts:

The following graph shows League debutants per year excepting those coming on as sub in the last game of the season (e.g. Simmons, O'Brien, Dudley):

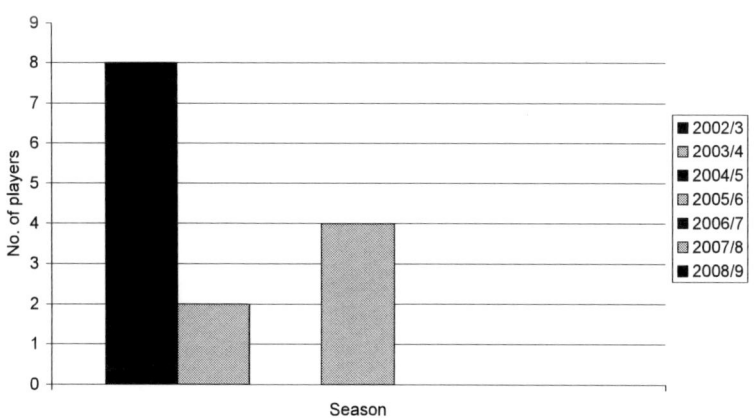

2002-3 Twigg, Tudgay, Grant, Hunt, McLeod, Mills, Holmes, Camp

2003-4 Huddlestone, Doyle,

2004-5 None

2005-6 Barnes, Nyatanga, Ainsworth, Addison

2006-7 None

2007-8 None

2008/9 None

It is also worth looking at the contribution of those players to show the role played by Rams produced players. The graph below shows league starts by homegrown players:

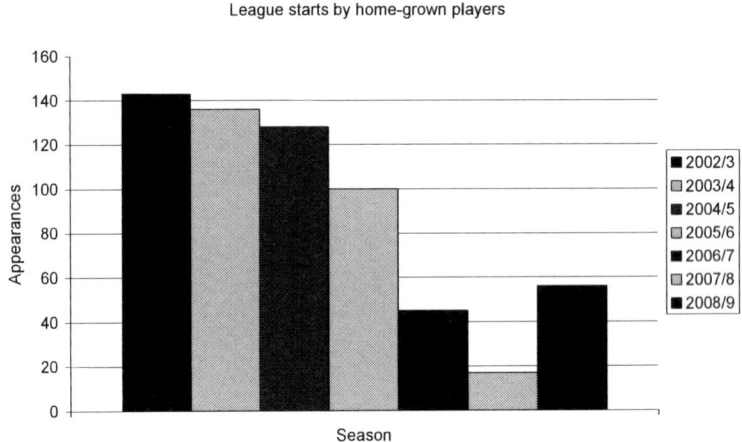

(Homegrown players used including those who appeared as substitute but not if only in final match!)

2002-3 Twigg, Tudgay, Grant, Hunt, McLeod, Mills, Holmes, Camp, Riggott, Elliott, Murray, Evatt, Robinson (13)

2003-4 Huddlestone, Holmes, Doyle, Tudgay, Grant, Mills, McLeod, Camp, Elliott (9)

2004-5 Huddlestone, Holmes, Doyle, Tudgay, Grant, Mills, Camp, (7)

2005-6 Barnes, Nyatanga, Addison, Holmes, Tudgay, Camp, Holmes, Mills, (8)

2006-7 Barnes, Nyatanga, Camp, Grant (4)

2007-8 Barnes, Nyatanga, Addison (3)

2008/9 Barnes, Nyatanga, Addison (3)

So what does this tell us?

The first and obvious point is that production seems to have dried up in the past few seasons. Or has it? With the absence of a reserve team it is difficult to know who is knocking on the door of the first team. One thing for sure is that both Davies and Jewell were very reluctant to introduce home-grown players. Although Jewell belatedly reintroduced Addison, it should be remembered that Jewell used and signed an astonishing number of players and Addison followed 20+ Jewell signings.

The great shame of all this is the amount of money spent on agents fees, loan fees, transfer fees and wages, when in some cases, all we needed to go was shout down the corridor. Let's take two recent examples: if we wanted someone to play right-wing a couple of time before deciding he wasn't up to it, why didn't we just play Paris Simmons instead of signing Pereplotkins? If we wanted a young defender to be our fifth sub, why not use under-contract Jason Beardsley or Mitch Hanson instead of signing Seb Hines (a player signed on loan from Middlesbrough by Chris Hutchings who failed to appear in a single match for The Rams)?

Consider this: Tudgay, Grant, Hunt, McLeod, Mills, Holmes, Camp, Ainsworth, Evatt and Doyle have all made careers for themselves at Championship level or below. The total amount of money we received for these players is less than we paid for the season loan of Kazmierczak (excepting the sell-on clause for McLeod). The theory that the grass is always greener, when it comes to signing players, has held sway for years and cost The Rams a small fortune.

Fortunately, Clough is trying to do something about it with the new development side. Young, hungry players who won't cost the earth and could supplement the first team squad when required. If you consider the contribution of Davis and Todd for the past couple of years – and the huge expense incurred

– it makes perfect sense for someone like Jake Buxton to be playing the kind of bit-part role latterly held by Todd and Davis. If he performs as poorly as the aforementioned pair, there's nothing lost. If he's up to it, we've got a Championship standard player for nothing.

So here's to another new era of development, let's just hope it brings us a player or two.

"Dad, Who's Pereplotkins?"

Also available from Pure Phase Publishing

BAD WORSE WORST
The Story of Derby County's Record Breaking 2007/8 Season

Written comments to the author regarding Bad Worse Worst:

"I stumbled across this book while on Amazon (as you do) and I'd just like to say what an excellent read it was."

"Just returned from my Easter trip to England, bringing your book with me. Spent this morning reading it through, and must say I liked it very much. Sad isn´t it? Enjoying reading about last season :-(. Anyway: Thanks for the good work. Hopefully there will be another one after this season?"

"I have just finished reading 'Bad, Worse, Worst' which I received as a Christmas present from my son and I thought it was excellent, I couldn't put it down once I started reading it. By the way, have they added Kit-Kats to the picture boards outside Pride Park of banned articles that you can't take into the ground yet?"

"A cracking read, I was laughing out loud at my desk"

"Got the book as a Christmas present. Thoroughly enjoying it, a great read. Thanks and more power to your elbow."

"I mean this in the best possible way, but it's cracking toilet reading!"

"Just got a copy of the book for my birthday - already I'm laughing (through the tears). Excellent work."

"…funny as ****!"

"I didn't see my husband for two days whilst he was reading it!"

Available at www.purephase-publishing.co.uk and all major on-line retailers